Microsoft
Pocket
Guide
to
Microsoft®
Access 2000

Microsoft Office Application

Stephen L. Nelson

Microsoft Press

PUBLISHED BY
Microsoft Press
A Division of Microsoft Corporation
One Microsoft Way
Redmond, Washington 98052-6399

Library of Congress Cataloging-in-Publication Data
Nelson, Stephen L., 1959-
    Microsoft Pocket Guide to Microsoft Access 2000 / Stephen L.
Nelson.
        p. cm.
    Includes index.
    ISBN 1-57231-969-0
    1. Database management.   2. Microsoft Acess.   I. Title.
QA76.9.D3N466   1999
005.75'65--dc21

                                                    98-44827
                                                    CIP

Printed and bound in the United States of America.

    3 4 5 6 7 8 9   MLML   4 3 2 1 0 9

Distributed in Canada by ITP Nelson, a division of Thomson Canada Limited.

A CIP catalogue record for this book is available from the British Library.

Microsoft Press books are available through booksellers and distributors worldwide. For further information about international editions, contact your local Microsoft Corporation office or contact Microsoft Press International directly at fax (425) 936-7329. Visit our Web site at mspress.microsoft.com.

Acquisitions Editor: Susanne M. Forderer
Project Editor: Anne Taussig

Microsoft
Pocket
Guide

to
Microsoft®
Access 2000

Microsoft Office Application

The Microsoft Pocket Guide to Microsoft Access 2000 *is divided into five sections. These sections are designed to help you find the information you need quickly.*

1 Environment

Terms and ideas you'll want to know to get the most out of Microsoft Access. All the basic parts of Access are shown and explained. The emphasis here is on quick answers, but many topics are cross-referenced so that you can find out more if you want to.

Diagrams of key components, with quick definitions, cross-referenced to more complete information.

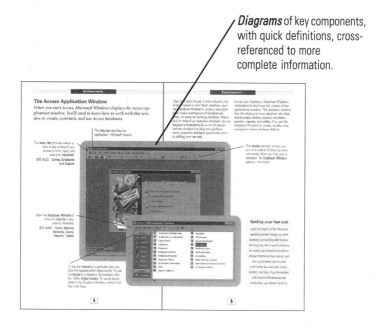

Tips

Watch for these as you use this Pocket Guide. They'll point out helpful hints and let you know what to watch for.

15 Access A to Z

An alphabetic list of commands, tasks, terms, and procedures.

Definitions of key concepts and terms, and examples showing you why you should know them.

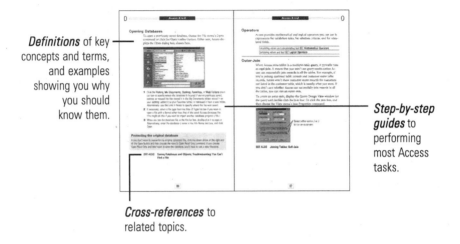

Step-by-step guides to performing most Access tasks.

Cross-references to related topics.

135 Troubleshooting

A guide to common problems—how to avoid them, and what to do when they occur.

149 Quick Reference

Useful indexes, including a full list of menu commands, toolbar buttons, and more.

159 Index

A complete reference to all elements of the Pocket Guide.

Introduction

This Pocket Guide provides
quick, practical answers to
just about any question
you have about
Microsoft Access 2000.
To acquaint yourself
with this convenient and
easy-to-use book, take two
minutes now and read the
Introduction. It explains
how this unusual little
book works.

What Is a Pocket Guide?

One of the problems with larger books about computers is, quite frankly, their size. With a large book, you must typically sift through pages of information to find that one piece of information you need. Not only that, you have to contend with their physical size. It's rarely enjoyable and often not practical to lug around a thousand-page book if you're working both at home and at the office, or if you're on the road with your laptop.

Microsoft Pocket Guide to Microsoft Access 2000 addresses both "size" problems of the larger computer books. Most obvious, of course, is the fact that this book is smaller. So it's easier to carry the book around wherever you go.

But this Pocket Guide also addresses the problem of wading through a large book to find the piece of information you need. And it does so in a variety of ways. For starters, this Pocket Guide organizes its information alphabetically, just like a dictionary or an encyclopedia does. This Pocket Guide supplies visual indexes in its Environment section, so you can find help even if you don't know how to describe what it is you're looking for. Finally, this Pocket Guide also uses a rich cross-referencing scheme that points you to related topics. For new users, the Pocket Guide provides the essential information necessary to start using Access. And for experienced users, the Pocket Guide provides concise, easy-to-find descriptions of Access tasks, terms, and techniques.

When You Have a Question

Let me explain how to find the information you need. If Access is new to you, flip first to the Environment section, which is a visual index. Find the picture that shows what you want to do or the task you have a question about. For example, if you want to know how to store information in a table, flip to pages 6 and 7, which show a table.

Next read the captions that describe the parts of the picture. Suppose that you're new to the business of creating databases and want to become familiar with database terms, such as rows and columns. The window on pages 6 and 7 has captions that describe the parts of a table, including its rows and columns.

You'll notice that some captions use **boldface** terms or are followed by additional boldface terms. These refer to entries in the second section, Access A to Z, and provide more information related to the caption's contents.

Access A to Z is a dictionary of more than 200 entries that define terms and describe tasks. (After you've worked with Access a little or if you're already an experienced user, you'll often be able to turn directly to that section.) So if you have just read the caption in the Environment section which says that tables can be joined with common fields, for example, you can flip to the **Joining Tables** entry in Access A to Z.

When an entry in Access A to Z appears as a term within an entry, I'll show it in **boldface** the first time it appears in that entry. For example, as part of describing what an Access database is, I tell you that a database includes query objects. In this case, the word **query** appears in bold letters, alerting you to the presence of a query entry. If you don't understand the term or want to do some brushing up, you can flip to the entry for more information.

When You Have a Problem

The third section, Troubleshooting, describes problems that new or casual users of Access often encounter. Following each problem description, I list one or more solutions you can employ to fix the problem.

When You Wonder About a Command

The Quick Reference at the end of the Pocket Guide describes the menu commands and toolbar buttons. If you want to know what a specific command or toolbar button does, turn to the Quick Reference. Don't forget about the Index either. You can look there to find all references in this book to any single topic.

Conventions Used Here

I have developed some conventions to make using this book easier for you. Rather than use wordy phrases, such as "Activate the File menu, and then choose the Print command" to describe how you choose a command, I'm just going to say, "Choose the File menu's Print command."

Here's another convention: to make dialog box button and box labels stand out, I've capitalized the initial letter of each word in the label. I think that this method makes it easier to understand an instruction such as "Select the Print To File check box." It's easier to see, for example, that "Print To File" is a label.

One final point: I generally try to tell you the easiest, most direct way to get things done. For example, I'll often suggest that you use **shortcut menu** commands or toolbar buttons rather than conventional menu commands. I also assume that you know how to select menu commands, windows, and dialog box elements by using either the mouse or the keyboard.

Environment

Need to get oriented
quickly? Then the
Environment is the place
to start. It defines the key
terms you'll need to know
and the core ideas you
should understand as
you begin exploring
Microsoft Access 2000.

What Is a Database?

A database is a collection of related information.

In a **paper-based database,** you might store information all over the place—for example, in filing cabinet drawers or even on top of your desk. This system makes using the information and keeping it up-to-date difficult.

SEE ALSO Forms; Query; Reports

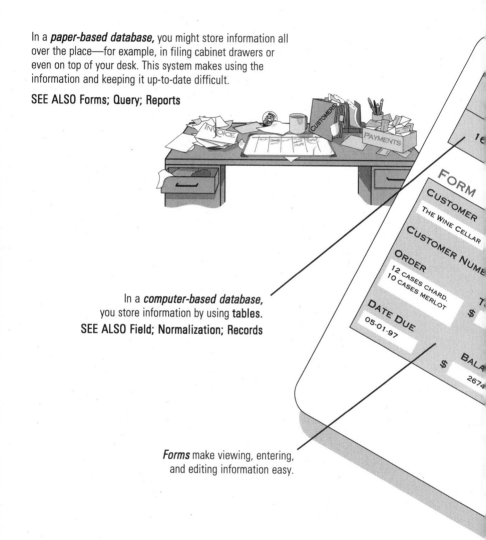

In a *computer-based database,* you store information by using **tables.**
SEE ALSO Field; Normalization; Records

Forms make viewing, entering, and editing information easy.

Database managers, such as Microsoft Access, provide tools that let you store database information. These managers also provide tools that make it easier to use and update the information in a database.

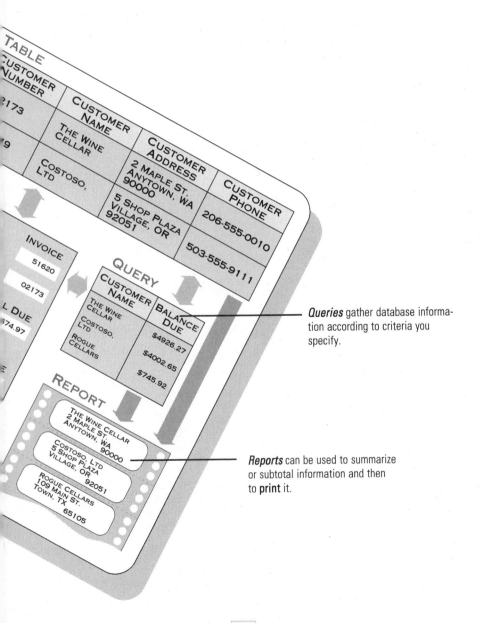

Queries gather database information according to criteria you specify.

Reports can be used to summarize or subtotal information and then to **print** it.

3

The Access Application Window

When you start Access, Microsoft Windows displays the Access application window. You'll need to know how to work with this window to create, maintain, and use Access databases.

The *title bar* identifies the application—Microsoft Access.

The *menu bar* provides menus, or lists, of the commands you choose to build, open, and save your **database**.
SEE ALSO Saving Databases and Objects

Open the *Database Window* to show the **objects** in your existing database.
SEE ALSO Forms; Macros; Modules; Query; Reports; Tables

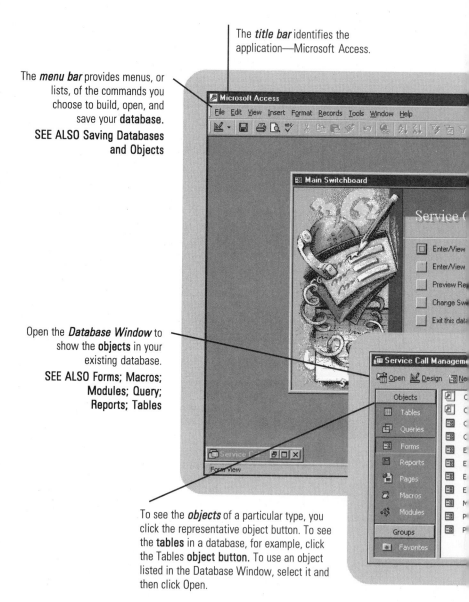

To see the *objects* of a particular type, you click the representative object button. To see the **tables** in a database, for example, click the Tables **object button**. To use an object listed in the Database Window, select it and then click Open.

After you start Access, it asks whether you want to create a new blank database, start the **Database Wizard** to create a new database (and a starting set of database **objects**), or open an existing database. When you've created or opened a database, Access displays a **Switchboard**—a set of menus custom-designed to help you perform many common database operations, such as adding new **records.**

Access also displays a **Database Window,** minimized in the lower left corner of the application window. The Database Window lists the objects in your database; the **data access pages, forms, macros, modules, queries, reports,** and **tables.** You use the Database Window to create, modify, and manipulate these database objects.

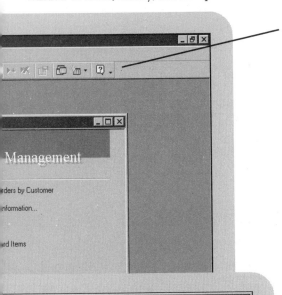

The *toolbar* provides buttons you can click instead of choosing menu commands. When you first open a database, the **Database Window** appears, minimized.

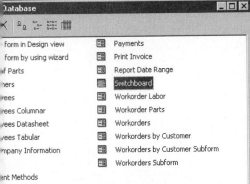

Getting your feet wet

Learn the basics of the Windows operating system before you start learning and working with Access. Although you don't need to become an expert, you should know how to choose commands from menus, and you should know how to work with dialog box elements: boxes, buttons, and lists. If you've worked with another Windows-based application, you almost certainly possess this core knowledge. If you haven't, I encourage you to read the first few chapters of the Windows user documentation.

Working with Tables

In a relational database, you store the information you collect in tables.

Tables organize database information into columns and rows. An Access database usually includes at least one table, but can include many. You create tables by clicking the Database Window's Table button and then the New button.
SEE ALSO Importing Data; Normalization

Rows contain your table entries, or **records**. For example, a customer database might have a **table** that lists customer addresses. In this table, each customer address is entered in its own row.

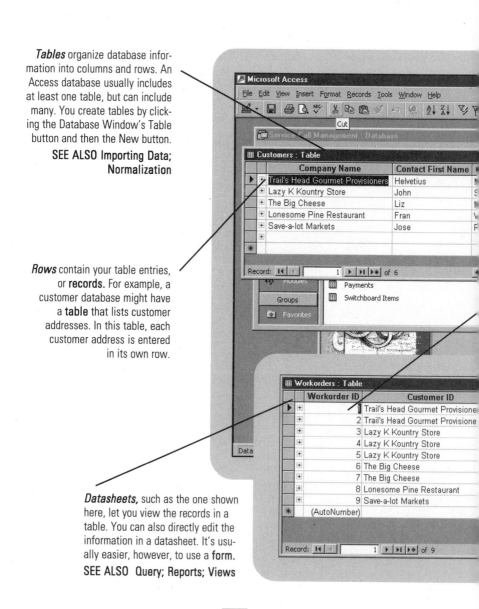

Datasheets, such as the one shown here, let you view the records in a table. You can also directly edit the information in a datasheet. It's usually easier, however, to use a **form**.
SEE ALSO Query; Reports; Views

Database creation begins with the description of the **table** or tables you'll use to store information. Typically, you'll use either the **Database Wizard** or the **Table Wizard** to create your tables. You can also create your tables from scratch, by individually describing the columns, or **fields,** that the table uses to store information.

After you describe the fields, you begin entering data in the table one row, or **record,** at a time. You can enter data directly in a table by using **datasheets** or indirectly by using a **form.**

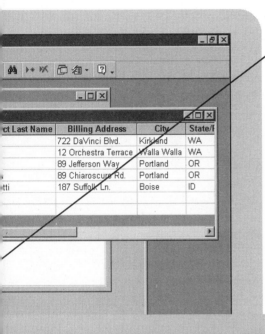

Columns organize the data in each record into *fields.* For example, in a table of work order data, the date on which each order was processed might be entered in a single column. In describing a table column, you also describe the type of data that can be stored in the column—text, numbers, and dates, for example.

SEE ALSO Data Types; Field Property; Validation Rules

Common fields let you join tables so that they can be combined in a query or for forms and reports.

SEE ALSO Index; Joining Tables; Primary Key; Referential Integrity; Relationships

ct Last Name	Billing Address	City	State/F
	722 DaVinci Blvd.	Kirkland	WA
	12 Orchestra Terrace	Walla Walla	WA
	89 Jefferson Way	Portland	OR
	89 Chiaroscuro Rd.	Portland	OR
tti	187 Suffolk Ln.	Boise	ID

Employee ID	PO	Date Received	Make/Model
Davolio, Nancy	1	11/23/94	ABC Cash Register 100
Fuller, Andrew	2	11/30/94	XYZ Cash Register 200
Peacock, Margaret	3	1/11/95	ABC Cash Register 300
Davolio, Nancy	5	1/18/95	XYZ Cash Register 100
Fuller, Andrew	6	1/25/95	ABC Cash Register 300
Leverling, Janet	4	1/12/95	XYZ Cash Register 300
Fuller, Andrew	8	2/2/95	ABC Cash Register 100
Davolio, Nancy	7	2/1/95	XYZ Cash Register 300
Buchanan, Steven	9	2/8/95	ABC Cash Register 100

Design your database on paper first

Before you start creating tables, sketch out which tables your **database** will need and which fields each table should have. You'll save yourself time in the long run.

7

Working with Forms

After you describe the tables in a database, you can enter records in the tables by using a form.

Entering a record with a form requires that you simply fill in each of the text boxes.

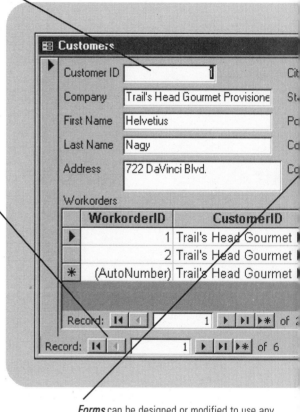

Editing a record requires that you first find the record and then make the changes by using the text boxes. Use these buttons to move backward and forward through a table's or a query's records.

Forms can be designed or modified to use any element of the Windows user interface.
SEE ALSO Control Wizards; Macro Buttons

A **form,** which is another type of database **object,** lets you enter, view, and print information from a **table** or a **query.** You can create simple forms quickly by using the Form Wizard. You can also create forms from scratch.

Although often used to enter data in tables, forms aren't limited to data entry and data editing. You can also use forms to view the data in a table or a query.

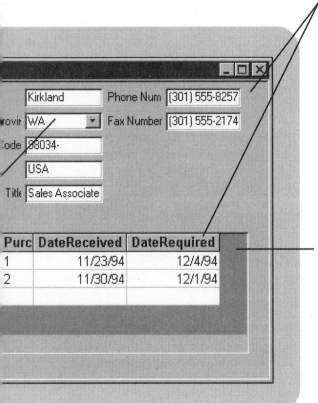

Main/Subforms let you work with a record from one **table** or **query** and all the related **records** from another table or query. Access lets you create other types of forms, including those that let you view or enter only one record at a time and those that display **graphs.**

The *Subform* shows the records related to the main form record.

9

Working with Queries

A query is a question you ask about data in your database. For example, "Who are my customers?" is a query.

Dynasets display the results of a query. A dynaset, then, is the answer to your question. This dynaset would answer the question "What total payments have been received for each customer?"

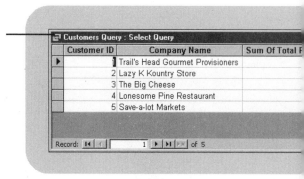

Joining tables during a query makes it possible to combine tables. To combine tables, the tables must use a **common field.**
SEE ALSO Equi-Join; Outer-Join; Primary Table; Relationships

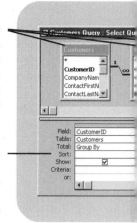

Sort orders, which you specify as part of describing the query, determine how query results are organized.
SEE ALSO Index; Primary Key

To ask a question about the data in your **database,** you need to describe the question, or query, in precise detail by creating a query **object.**

You can ask Access to summarize, organize, and even update database information as it answers your question. For example, you can tell Access to count the number of customers in a customer **table.** You can tell Access to total the amounts customers owe, and you can tell it to calculate a finance charge and add this charge to the amount a customer owes.

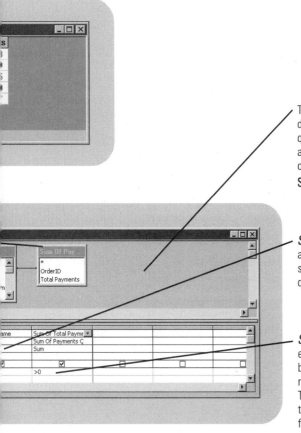

The *Design view* of a query object describes in precise detail the question the query asks, including any selection criteria, sort orders, or totals you want calculated.
SEE ALSO Views

Subtotals can be easily added to a query by telling Access how it should group and summarize query results.

Selection criteria are often essential to answering the query because they determine which records appear in the **dynaset.** This selection criteria tells Access that you want to see information for only customers with total payments greater than zero.
SEE ALSO Filter; Logical Operators

11

Printing Database Information

You can print information from or about any of the objects in a database. You can, for example, print a table to show its contents or print a query's dynaset to show the answer to the question the query asks.

Reports are another type of database **object**. You display an on-screen version of the report by opening the report object. When you do, Access displays the Print Preview window that shows how the report's pages look.

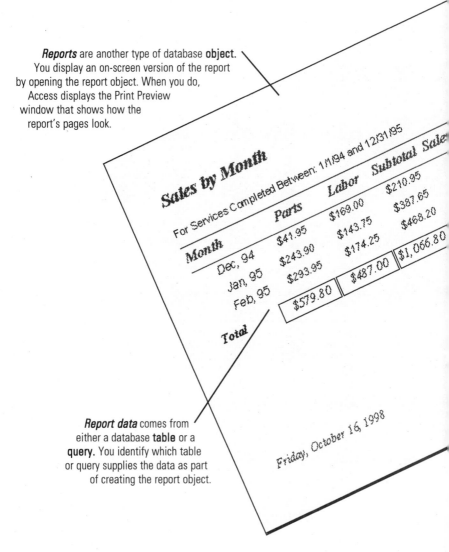

Report data comes from either a database **table** or a **query**. You identify which table or query supplies the data as part of creating the report object.

Although you can print the information shown in a table or a query by simply clicking the Print toolbar button, you can also create **reports** to organize, summarize, and format the information in a single **table** or a single **query.**

The easiest way to create a report is by using the Report Wizard, which steps you through a series of dialog boxes that ask about the information you want to see and how it should be organized.

SEE ALSO Mailing Labels

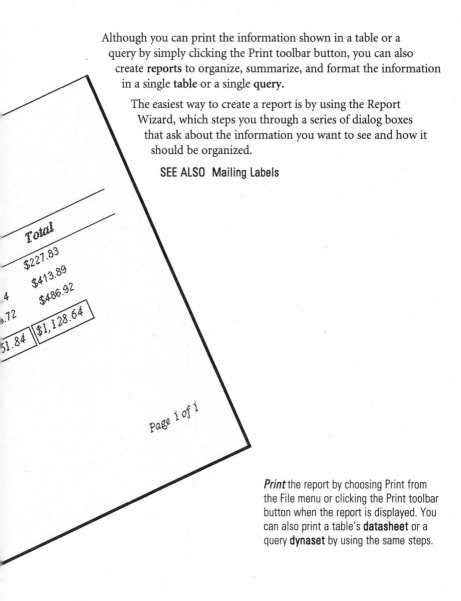

Print the report by choosing Print from the File menu or clicking the Print toolbar button when the report is displayed. You can also print a table's **datasheet** or a query **dynaset** by using the same steps.

Access

A to Z

When you have a question,
you want a quick, easy answer.
Access A to Z,
which starts on the next
page, provides just these
sorts of answers.
It lists in alphabetic order
the tools, terms, and
techniques you'll
need to know.

Access Basic SEE Visual Basic

Action Query

An action query is a **query** that changes or deletes data in the queried **tables**—for example, a query that calculates customer finance charges and adds these amounts to the customer balances. Microsoft Access provides four types of action queries: update, append, delete, and make table. In the paragraphs that follow, I'll briefly describe how each one works.

Creating and Running Update Action Queries

An update action query changes table **records**. To create an update query:

1 Create a **select query** that selects only the records you want to change.

2 Choose the View menu's Design View command, or click **View** to switch to Design view.

3 Choose the Query menu's Update Query command. Access changes the object window name to Update Query and adds a new row titled Update To.

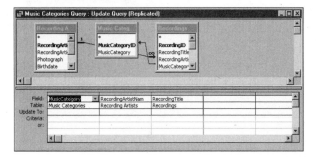

4 Enter the value or the text (or the expression that returns the value or the text) in the appropriate Update To cells. Then run the query in the usual way. (If you want to test your action query before you run it for real, click View.)

Testing action queries

If you haven't run an action query: (1) run some tests on sample data to make sure that your action query works the way it's supposed to; (2) **back up** your **database** before you run the action query just in case something bad happens or you ignore my first suggestion; (3) click View to preview the effects of your action query.

Creating and Running Append Action Queries

You can add, or append, to an existing table the query results shown in a **dynaset**. Follow these steps:

1 Create and run the select query that produces a dynaset with the records you want to add.

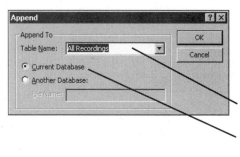

2 Click the View toolbar button to switch to Design view.

3 Choose the Query menu's Append Query command. Access displays the Append dialog box.

4 Identify the table to which records should be added.

5 Identify the database in which the table is an object.

6 Click OK to close the Append dialog box.

7 Choose the Query menu's Run command or click Run.

Creating and Running Delete Action Queries

You can delete from the queried tables the query results shown in a dynaset. Before you run a delete query, however, you should back up your data. When you've backed it up, follow these steps to run your delete query:

1 Create and run the select query that produces a dynaset with the records you want to delete.

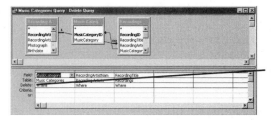

2 Click the View toolbar button to switch to Design view.

3 Choose the Query menu's Delete Query command. Access adds a Delete row to the query design grid and changes the object window title bar to Delete Query.

4 Choose the Query menu's Run command, or click Run.

continues

Action Query *(continued)*

Creating and Running Make-Table Action Queries

You can add to a new table the query results shown in a dynaset. Follow these steps:

1 Create and run the select query that produces a dynaset with the records you want to add to the new table.

2 Click the View toolbar button to switch to Design view.

3 Choose the Query menu's Make-Table Query command. Access displays the Make Table dialog box.

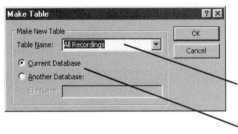

4 Identify the new table to which the records should be added.

5 Identify the database in which the new table should be an object.

6 Click OK to close the Make Table dialog box.

7 Choose the Query menu's Run command, or click Run.

Saving an Action Query

You can save an action query in the same manner you save a select query. When you close the query object window, for example, Access will ask whether you want to save the query. If you answer yes and provide a query name, Access will add the query as an object to your database.

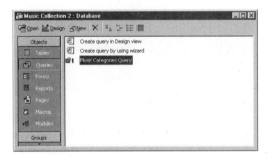

Because action queries change data, Access sticks an exclamation point in front of the query object name in the **Database Window**. Remember: opening one of these action queries may change your data!

Active and Inactive Windows

The active **document window** is the one you see in the **program window**. Any commands you choose affect the **document** in the active document window.

The active application window—such as the Access program window—is the one that appears in front of any other application windows on your screen—in the foreground. The inactive program windows, if there are inactive programs, appear in the background.

Opening Program Windows

You can open a different program window by clicking the window or the application's button on the Taskbar.

Opening Document Windows

You can open a different document window by either clicking the window or choosing the Window menu's command naming that window.

Adaptability

Access customizes its menus so that they supply only the commands you choose and its toolbars so that they provide only the tools you use. This adaptability makes it easier for you to find the menu commands and toolbar buttons you regularly use.

You still have access to all Access features even with its adaptability, however. If you point to the double arrow at the bottom of a menu or linger on a menu, Access displays its long menus, which supply all your commands. If you click the double-arrow toolbar button, you display an extended set of toolbar buttons.

SEE ALSO   Personal Menus and Toolbars

ASCII Text Files

An ASCII text file is simply a **file** that uses only ASCII characters. You can import an ASCII text file into database applications such as Access by choosing the File menu's Import command and the submenu's Get External Data command.

Sharing data among programs

A last-resort method for sharing data among programs is to create an ASCII text file. This technique works because many programs—spreadsheets, databases, and accounting programs, among others—produce text files.

SEE ALSO   **Importing Data**

AutoCorrect

AutoCorrect seeks out and corrects many types of common data-entry errors as you work, including errors in spelling, nonstandard capitalization, and more. For instance, if you misspell the word *the* as *teh*, AutoCorrect fixes your mistake.

SEE ALSO   **AutoCorrect Options**

AutoCorrect Options

Although **AutoCorrect** works great as the Access Setup program installs it, you can fine-tune its operation. To change the way AutoCorrect works, follow these steps:

1 Choose the Tools menu's AutoCorrect command.

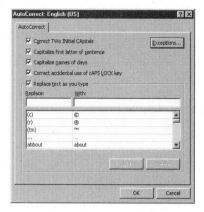

2 Select check boxes in the AutoCorrect dialog box for the corrections you want Access to make.

3 To augment the Access list of commonly misspelled words, type the misspelling in the Replace box, and then type the correct spelling in the With box.

4 Click Add to add the misspelled word/correctly spelled word combination to the list box.

5 Click OK when you're finished.

AutoForm Wizard

The AutoForm Wizard will build a **form** for you automatically. All you need to do is display the **table** or the **query** datasheet for which you want to create a form, click New Object so that Access displays a drop-down list of objects you can create, and then click AutoForm.

AutoNumber

An AutoNumber is a **field** that Access fills in for you. (In earlier versions of Access, AutoNumber fields were called counter fields.) Typically, you use AutoNumber fields to assign unique identification numbers to the **records** in a **table**. In this case, the Auto-Number field is the **primary key** and, most probably, a **common field** if you are **joining tables**.

continues

AutoNumber *(continued)*

If an AutoNumber field is a common field

If you want to use the identification numbers created by an AutoNumber field as the common field between two tables, the identification number in the other, nonprimary table must have its **data type** specified as Long Integer.

AutoReport

AutoReport will build a report for you automatically. All you need to do is display the **table** or **query** datasheet for which you want to create a **report,** click New Object so that Access displays a drop-down list of objects you can create, and then click AutoReport.

Back Up

The easiest way to back up **database** files is to copy them to a floppy disk. If you want to make your task slightly easier and you have a handful of files, you may also be able to use the Microsoft Backup program. This isn't a book about Windows, so I won't describe here how the Backup application works. You'll need to refer to the Windows user documentation.

If you have a great deal of information to back up—such as a 50MB database file—you'll want to back up to a tape, a removable hard disk, or a network drive. For that task, you'll need to use the Backup application. One more thing: Access database files use the file extension MDB; Access add-in files use the file extension MDA; Access add-in data files use the file extension MDT; and Access workgroup files use the file extension MDW. Those extensions are handy to know when you back up files.

Bound Object Frames

Suppose that you have a database of employee information and you want to build a **data access page** that includes a photo of each employee. Access allows you to embed or link the photos (as bitmap files, for example) into the employee information **table.** To have those photos appear on the data access page (or a **form**), you need to insert a bound object frame from the **toolbox.** For more information, see your user documentation.

SEE ALSO   Embedding and Linking Objects; Object; OLE Objects

Calculated Controls

Calculated controls are **control objects** that calculate **expressions.** These controls sometimes appear on **forms,** and they always appear on **reports** that summarize data.

Calculated Fields

You can add a calculated field to a **query** or a **form.**

Calculating a Value for a Query

To calculate a value for a query, follow these steps:

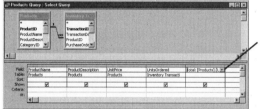

1 Select the column of the query design window in which the calculated field should be placed.

2 Enter the calculated field name followed by a colon.

3 Enter a formula that describes the calculation. In this case, unit price is being multiplied by units ordered.

You can use **field names** (but not calculated field names) in calculated fields as long as you include them in brackets [ ]. You can use any of the Access **mathematical operators;** you can use values; and you can also use **functions.**

Concatenating Text

You can concatenate, or combine, separate **fields** in a query by using the & (concatenation) operator. For example, if you've stored a person's last and first names in two separate fields, you can combine them, with a space between each name, by using this **expression:** Name:[First Name]&" "&[Last Name].

Limiting the Records Used in a Calculation

You can limit, or restrict, which **records'** fields are used in a calculation by using the Where summary **operator.** Enter the operator Where into the Total row of the query design grid. Then enter the criteria that selects the records you want to include.

Clipboard

When you're working with Windows or a Windows-based **program,** you can use the Clipboard to move blocks of text, **tables,** and even graphics images to and from different **files.** You can also use the Clipboard to move text, tables, and graphics images between Windows applications, such as from Paint to Access. To move information around via the Clipboard, you use the Edit menu's Cut, Copy, and Paste commands or the Cut, Copy, and Paste buttons on your toolbar.

The Windows 95 Clipboard holds only one edit at a time—each time you copy or cut something, the previous Clipboard contents are replaced.

Office 2000 includes a Clipboard toolbar. If you copy or cut more than one selection to the Clipboard, the toolbar pops up. It shows how many items you've stored on the Clipboard. If you don't see the Clipboard toolbar, you can choose the View menu's Toolbars command and the submenu's Clipboard command.

If you choose the Edit menu's Paste command or click the Paste toolbar button, Access copies the most recent addition from the Clipboard. You can use the Clipboard toolbar to copy an addition other than the most recent one, however. Click the picture representing the selection you want to copy. If you don't know which Clipboard picture represents which copied or cut selection, point to the picture. Windows will display a pop-up box describing the Clipboard contents. Two final, quick notes about the Clipboard toolbar: You can click its Paste All button to paste into the active document everything you've stored on the Clipboard, and you can click the Clipboard toolbar's Clear Clipboard button to erase the Clipboard.

Closing Database Objects

You close database objects so they don't consume memory and clutter your screen. To close a single database object, either click its Close button or be sure that the object is the active window and then choose the File menu's Close command.

If you have unsaved changes

Access won't close an object to which you have made design changes but not yet **saved.** It will first ask whether you want to save your design changes.

Closing Databases

You close a **database** file by **exiting Access** or by opening a new database file. (Because you can have only one database file open, Access closes the first database file before it opens the next database file.) You don't need to save changes to the data in the database file. Access does that automatically.

Common Fields

Common fields are the **fields** that **tables** in a **database** share. If your database is correctly designed, you probably use common fields to connect, or **join,** tables. (If a common field isn't being used to join tables, it might indicate a data redundancy.)

Common field names and properties

It's a good idea to use the same name for common fields. Identical names make it easy for Access to join the tables. Common fields should use the same **field properties** in each table in which they appear, with one exception: if you use an **AutoNumber** field in one table, the same field in the other table should be a number with the Long Integer data type if the two tables have a one-to-many relationship.

Comparison Operators SEE Logical Operators

Concatenation Operators SEE Mathematical Operators

Control Menu Commands

Control menu commands appear on the Control menus of **application windows,** object windows, and dialog boxes.

To open the Control menu, click the Control menu icon (the small icon in the upper left corner of the window or the dialog box).

Control menu commands let you manipulate the window or the dialog box in the following ways:

Restore

Undoes the last minimize or maximize command.

Move

Allows you to move the window or the dialog box. The mouse pointer changes to a four-headed arrow. When this happens, use the Up and Down arrow keys to change the screen position of the window or the dialog box.

Size

Allows you to resize the window. The mouse pointer changes to a four-headed arrow. Use the Up and Down arrow keys to move the top or bottom border and the Left and Right arrow keys to move the left or right border.

Minimize

Removes the window from the screen. To remind you of the minimized window, Windows displays a button on the Taskbar.

Maximize

Makes the window or the dialog box as big as possible. In the case of a window, this would cover the whole screen.

Close

Closes the window or the dialog box. If you close a program window, it's the same as choosing the File menu's Exit command. If you made changes that haven't yet been **saved,** Access will ask whether you want to save the changes. Closing a dialog box is the same as clicking Cancel.

About the Control menu commands

You won't always see all these commands on a Control menu. Windows displays only those that make sense in the current situation.

SEE ALSO Closing Databases; Switching Tasks

Control Objects

Control objects are the objects you see on a **form,** a **report,** or a **graph.** On a form, for example, the boxes and buttons that appear on the form as well as any labels that describe the form and its boxes and buttons are control objects.

Control Wizards

Control wizards help you create **control objects.** Because I don't get into the details of custom **form** and **report** design in this Pocket Guide, I don't spend much time discussing Control Wizards and control objects—except to explain how you use them to construct **macro buttons** for forms.

Converting Previous-Edition Access Files SEE Database

Counter SEE AutoNumber

Crosstab

You can cross-tabulate data as part of a **query.** A cross-tabulation tabulates, or summarizes, data in two ways. For example, you might want to summarize sales revenue by both state and product, as shown here.

In this cross-tabulation, Access uses rows to summarize units ordered by date, and columns to summarize units ordered by product type.

The row-column inter-sections show product type per date.

continues

Crosstab *(continued)*

A friendly suggestion

A crosstab is a powerful—and somewhat complex—tool. Before you try one, make a few of the simpler select queries.

Creating a Crosstab Query

To create a crosstab query, follow these steps:

1 Open the Database Window.

2 Click Queries.

3 Click New. Access displays the New Query dialog box.

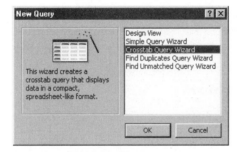

4 Choose the Crosstab Query Wizard, and click OK.

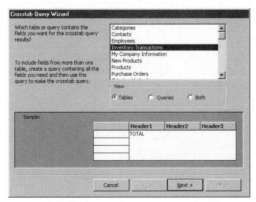

5 When Access displays the first Crosstab Query Wizard dialog box, indicate whether you want to see tables, queries, or both tables and queries by clicking one of the View option buttons.

6 Click to select the table or query you'll query.

7 Click Next.

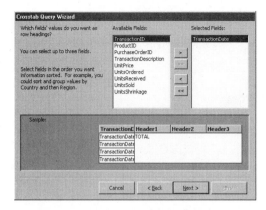

8 Add to the crosstab summary the fields you'll summarize in rows by double-clicking the fields to select them in the list box at the top of the dialog box. (You can select as many as three fields.)

9 Click Next.

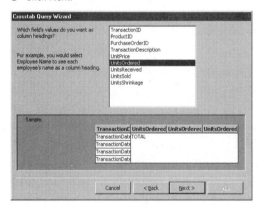

10 Add the fields you'll summarize in columns by selecting them in the list box at the top of the dialog box.

11 Click Next.

continues

Crosstab *(continued)*

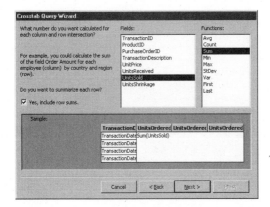

12 Specify what you want to summarize in the crosstab by selecting the field you want to summarize and the calculation you want to make.

13 To add a column that summarizes the totals by row, select the Yes, Include Row Sums check box.

14 Click Next.

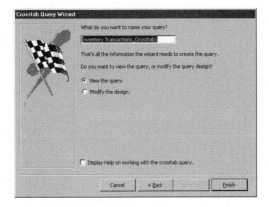

15 Give the crosstab query a name.

16 Click Finish. Access performs the crosstab query.

Data Access Page

Access enables you to build web pages to allow others to access your database on the Internet—the database becomes sort of a web-based **form.** For example, salespeople could enter or update purchase orders while they're on the road. To build a data access page, open a database, open the **Database Window,** and then click Pages. You can build a page from scratch, use a wizard, or edit an existing data access page.

SEE ALSO   Saving Data Access Pages

Database

A database is simply a collection of related information, or data. One common database is a telephone directory. It lists peoples' names, addresses, and telephone numbers, so it's a names-and-numbers database. In business, accounting programs create financial databases—lists of financial information, such as customer invoices, expenses, and items held as inventory.

In Access, the term *database* is defined more precisely. An Access database is composed of its database **objects,** or components: **tables, queries, forms, reports, macros,** and **modules.** Access stores in a single **file** the objects that constitute a database.

Creating a New Database File

To create a new database, follow these steps:

1 Choose the File menu's New command.

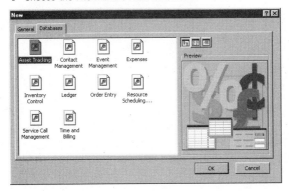

continues

Database *(continued)*

2 If you want to design a database from scratch, select the Database template on the General tab. If you want a wizard to help you, click the Databases tab and select one of the predesigned Access database templates.

3 Click OK. Access displays the File New Database dialog box.

4 Specify where the database should be saved in the Save In box.

5 Name the database in the File Name box.

6 Click Create. Access creates the database and, if you indicated that you wanted to use one of the database templates, starts the **Database Wizard.** (The Database Wizard lets you customize the tables by adding and removing **fields,** selecting a design style for your forms and reports, and naming the database. You make your database design decisions by clicking buttons and filling in text boxes.)

Opening an Existing Database File

To open a database file that already exists, follow these steps:

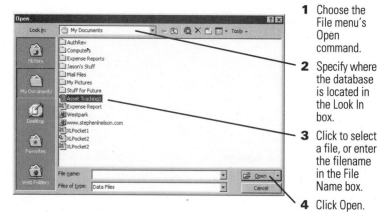

1 Choose the File menu's Open command.

2 Specify where the database is located in the Look In box.

3 Click to select a file, or enter the filename in the File Name box.

4 Click Open.

Using Databases Created with Previous Versions of Access

You'll need to convert databases created with any previous version of Access. To do this, follow these steps:

1 Close any open databases.

2 Choose the Tools menu's Database Utilities command and the submenu's Convert Database To Current Access Database Version command. Access displays a dialog box similar to the Open dialog box.

3 Identify the database file to be converted. Give the conversion a new name if you don't want the old file to be overwritten.

4 Click Convert.

Adding Data to a Database File

After you've created the database file, you're ready to begin either filling the tables with data or, if you started with a blank database, creating tables.

SEE ALSO   RDBMS

Database Window

The Database Window is the central repository for all the **objects** in a **database.** To access the Database Window, click the Database Window toolbar button or press F11.

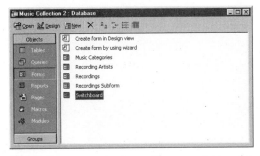

If you built your own database without a switchboard feature, the Database Window appears when you open an existing database. In databases with a switchboard, the Database Window is usually minimized in the lower left corner of the **program window.**

Double-click the minimized window to open it.

continues

Database Window *(continued)*

A tip for Windows Explorer users

The Database Window works in a manner very similar to Windows Explorer. With the Database Window, you can view database objects as icons or in detailed lists—use the View menu's Large Icons, Small Icons, List, or Details command. You can also drag-and-drop objects to copy and move them.

Database Wizard

The Database Wizard builds a database for you, including **tables, forms,** and **reports.** You can even have the Database Wizard add sample data you can experiment with to learn how to use Access faster.

Starting the Database Wizard

If you're just starting up Access, select the Access Database Wizards, Pages And Projects option. If the program is already running, choose the File menu's New command.

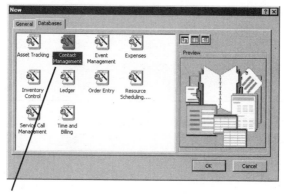

Select one of the 10 Access database templates, which are collections of database objects specifically designed to handle certain tasks. With a template, you can start entering and manipulating data right away.

Using the Database Wizard

When you use the Database Wizard, you indicate which fields you want in the various tables it creates; you specify how you want the on-screen forms and reports to look—their layout, fonts, and colors; and you name the database.

I'll describe the steps you take to use the Database Wizard, but because the Database Wizard is so easy to use, you might want to experiment by creating a sample database or two.

To use the Database Wizard, follow these steps:

1 Select a database template, and then click OK.

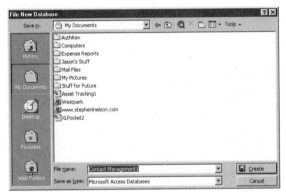

2 Name your database in the File Name box. You can also use the Save In box to specify where the database should be saved.

3 Click Create. Access creates a database file and then displays a Database Wizard dialog box that identifies what sort of information you'll be able to store in the database.

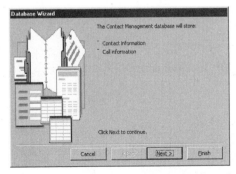

4 If you want Access to make all the decisions about the database design, click Finish. Otherwise, click Next.

continues

Database Wizard *(continued)*

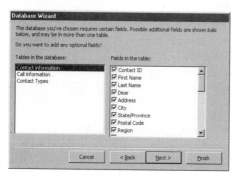

5 Under Tables In The Database, select each table in turn and, using the Fields In The Table list box, select the fields you want. Click Next.

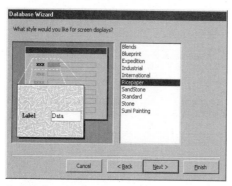

6 Select a style for your on-screen displays. Note that this step will not affect your printed reports. Click Next.

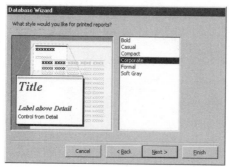

7 Select a style for your printed reports. Click Next.

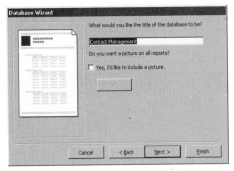

8 Give your database a name. This name is not the same as the filename, by the way. It's the name that Access will use on the **switchboard,** a menu you'll use to work with your new database.

You can also choose a picture to include on all reports. Select the Yes, I'd Like To Include A Picture check box. Then click Picture, and use the Insert Picture dialog box to identify the picture file and its location. Click Next.

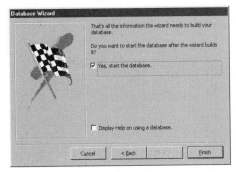

9 Choose whether you want to start the database after it's built and whether you'll want help right away. Click Finish. That's it!

Datasheet

Access uses a datasheet to display **table** records and **query** results on-screen. You can enter data directly into a datasheet.

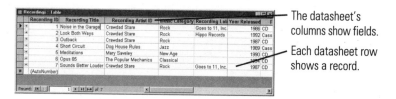

The datasheet's columns show fields.

Each datasheet row shows a record.

Printing a Datasheet

Choose the File menu's Print command. When Access displays the Print dialog box, use its options to specify how the datasheet should be printed. Or press Enter to accept the default, or suggested, options.

Changing Column Widths

You can change the width of a datasheet's columns by dragging the right edge of a column heading. Or choose the Format menu's Column Width command, and enter a width specification in characters.

Changing the column width automatically

You can tell Access that it should adjust a column width to the size of the longest entry by double-clicking the right edge of the column heading.

Moving Columns

You can move the selected column by dragging it to a new location.

Changing Row Heights

You can change the height of a datasheet's rows by dragging the bottom edge of any row heading. Or choose the Format menu's Row Height command, and enter a height specification in points. (One point equals 1/72 inch.)

Hiding and Unhiding Columns

You can hide a column so that it doesn't show in a datasheet. Select the column by clicking it, and then choose the Format menu's Hide Columns command.

To unhide columns you've hidden, choose the Format menu's Unhide Columns command. When Access displays the Unhide Columns dialog box, select the columns you want to unhide from the Column list box and then click Close.

Freezing Columns

You can freeze a column or multiple columns so that they don't scroll off the screen as you scroll to the right. Select the columns by clicking them, and then choose the Format menu's Freeze Columns command.

To unfreeze frozen columns, choose the Format menu's Unfreeze All Columns command.

Data Types

Data type refers to the characteristics of the information in a **field**. If the field contains textual information, such as someone's first name, the field is a text field—the field's data type is text. If a field contains a value you want to use in a calculation, the field is a number field. A field's data type may also limit the type of information you can enter. Access provides the following 10 data types:

Data type	What a field of this data type stores
Text	Anything you want as long as the field contains fewer than 255 characters.
Memo	Text—just like the text data type—except that this field will hold as many as 64,000 characters.
Number	A numeric value you may want to use in a calculation. A number field can't store alphabetic characters.
Date/Time	A calendar-and-clock value. Access automatically validates information you insert into Date/Time fields: whatever you enter into one of these fields must look like a date or time.
Currency	A numeric value with two decimal places. If you're working in the United States, for example, you'll use currency fields to store dollars and cents. If you're working in Great Britain, you'll use currency fields to store pounds and pence. A currency field isn't rounded off during calculation, which makes it accurate.

continues

Data Types *(continued)*

Data type	What a field of this data type stores
AutoNumber	A numeric value that Access calculates and fills in for you by adding one to the preceding **record's** AutoNumber counter. You use the AutoNumber field when you don't have another numbering scheme or system for uniquely identifying records.
Yes/No	A value that can equal only Yes or No. Yes can be indicated as *Yes, True,* or *On;* No can be indicated as *No, False,* or *Off.*
OLE Object	A field that can hold only an **OLE object**—for example, pictures created by the Paint accessory or sounds created by the Sound Recorder accessory.
Hyperlink	Text or combinations of text and numbers used as a hyperlink address—a link to another Access object, a Microsoft Office document, or a World Wide Web page.
Lookup Wizard	A list of a fixed set of values or a list that "looks up" data from an existing table or query.

SEE ALSO   **Validation Rules**

Why Access doesn't have calculation fields

You don't need fields for storing calculation results. Access will make calculations for you as you need them and then display the results in **dynasets** produced by **queries** and on **reports** and **forms.**

Default Values

When you design and redesign a **table,** you can tell Access to suggest a default entry for a **field.** You do this by using the Default Value **field property.** The following table lists some examples of default value settings and their effect.

Default value	Access suggestion
USA	If the data type is text, Access suggests USA.
1	If the data type is text, Access suggests the character 1. If the data type is number, Access suggests the value 1. If the data type is Yes/No, Access suggests the answer Yes.
0	If the data type is text, Access suggests the character 0. If the data type is number, Access suggests the value 0. If the data type is Yes/No, Access suggests the answer No.
=Date()	If the data type is Date/Time, Access suggests the current system date.
=Time()	If the data type is Date/Time, Access suggests the current system time.
=Now()	If the data type is Date/Time, Access suggests the current system date and time.

SEE ALSO   Expressions; Functions

Deleting Files SEE Erasing Databases

Design View SEE Views

Desktop

The desktop is what you see when you start Windows. It's the desktop, for example, that provides shortcut icons and on which the Start button and Taskbar rest. The desktop doesn't have anything to do directly with Access—except that both the Open Workbook and Save Workbook dialog boxes let you easily store and retrieve Access databases from there.

Detect And Repair

Microsoft Office 2000 programs such as Access provide a Detect And Repair command on their Help menus. You can choose this command to direct Access to look for and, if possible, repair problems with noncritical files. Note that Access automatically identifies and repairs problems with critical files.

Documents

In Windows-based programs, a document is what a **program** displays in the **Document Window**. In the case of a word processor, the use of the term *document* is self-evident.

Unfortunately, the "document" label doesn't work as well to name the windows and window contents that Access displays. What Access displays in the windows inside its program window are **views** of database **objects**. Nevertheless, Access labels these objects and object views as documents.

Document Window

A document window is the window in which a **program** such as Access displays the **views** of its database **objects.**

Dynaset

Dynaset is a shorthand expression for *dyna*mic sub*set*. When you query a **table** or another **query,** what gets displayed in the **datasheet** window is a dynamic subset, or a dynaset.

What makes a dynaset "dynamic" is that if you make a change to the information displayed in the datasheet window (because of the query), Access updates the tables that provided the raw information.

E-Mail

You can e-mail the active Access database to someone else. Choose the File menu's Send To, Mail Recipient (As Attachment) command. Windows starts your e-mail program and attaches the active database to the message. To complete the message, you typically just supply the recipient's e-mail name and click the Send toolbar button. Note that Access doesn't provide this command unless it knows that you have e-mail service.

Embedding and Linking Objects

Access lets you store more than numbers and portions of text in **tables.** It also lets you store **OLE** objects. (Don't confuse OLE objects with the **objects** that constitute a database.)

Embedding and Linking Existing Objects

To create an object from an existing **file,** follow these steps:

1 Place the insertion point in the field in which the object should be inserted. (The field's data type must be "OLE Object.")

2 Choose the Insert menu's Object command.

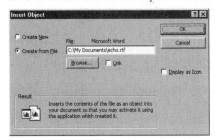

3 Click the Create From File option button.

4 Describe the object file location and identify the object file by using the File box. If you don't know the object's filename or location, click Browse. Then use the dialog box to specify the file.

5 Select the Display As Icon check box if you want Access to display an icon to represent the embedded object rather than the object itself.

6 Select the Link check box if you want Window to update the object for subsequent file changes.

7 Click OK.

continues

Embedding and Linking Objects *(continued)*

Embedding New Objects

To create an object from scratch, follow these steps:

1 Place the insertion point in the field in which the object should be inserted. The field's data type must be "OLE Object."

2 Choose the Insert menu's Object command.

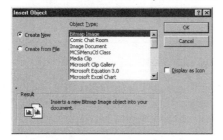

3 Click the Create New option button.

4 Select the Windows-based application you'll use to create the object.

5 Select the Display As Icon check box if you want Access to display an icon to represent the embedded object rather than the object itself.

6 Click OK. Access starts the selected application, allowing you to create the object.

7 When you're finished, exit the application.

Entering Text and Numbers

To enter text or numbers into a **form's** text box or into a **datasheet's** cell, select the text box or cell by clicking it or move from box to box or from cell to cell by pressing the Tab key, the Enter key, or the arrow keys. Then use the keyboard to type the characters.

In Access, you edit and erase text and numbers the same way you do in other Windows-based programs. Note, though, that the field's **data type** may limit what you can enter in a text box or cell.

SEE ALSO AutoCorrect

Equi-Join

Because Access runs an equi-join when it joins **tables** in a multiple-table **query,** you won't see query results unless Access can successfully join records in all the tables. For example, if you're joining customer table **records** and customer order table records, Access won't show customer order records for customers not listed in the customer table, which is usually what you want. You should know, however, that you can also run an **outer-join.**

SEE ALSO   Self-Join

Erasing Databases

Databases get stored as **files** on disk. To erase them in Windows, you use Windows Explorer or My Computer.

Erasing Files with Windows Explorer

To erase files after you've started Windows Explorer, follow these steps:

1 Select the folder or the subfolder that contains the files you want to erase.

2 Select the files you want to erase.

3 Choose the File menu's Delete command.

4 When Windows Explorer asks, confirm that you want to send the files to the Recycle Bin.

What's in a database file?

A database file contains all the **objects** that make up the database. The file doesn't contain **tables** that are only attached, however.

Exiting Microsoft Access

To exit from Access (and just about any other Windows-based **program**), choose the File menu's Exit command. Or you can close the **program window** by clicking the Close button (the X in the upper right corner) or the Control menu icon (the icon in the upper left corner of the application window). Access will ask whether you want to save **objects** that have unsaved layout changes. Note that Access automatically saves changes to data in tables.

SEE ALSO   Closing Databases; Saving Databases and Objects

Exporting Data

You can export data from Access and use it in a spreadsheet such as Microsoft Excel or in a word processor such as Microsoft Word. Here's the easiest and quickest way:

1 Select a **report** that shows the data you want to export in the way you want it exported. Or open the **table** with the data you want to export.

2 Choose the File menu's Export command.

3 Use the Save As Type drop-down list box to select an output format that can be imported by the **application** you want to use. (Use Rich Text Format for exporting to a word processor like Word.)

4 Specify a filename for the new exported file in the File Name box.

5 Specify where the file should be located in the Save In box.

6 Click Save.

Outputting to Excel or to Word

You can use the Office Links commands—Merge It Or Publish It With MS Word and Analyze It With MS Excel—to export Access reports to Excel and Word.

Expressions

An expression is simply a formula. You can use expressions to return **default values** for input **fields** in **datasheets** and **forms.** You can use expressions for **calculated fields** in **queries.** You can use expressions to validate field entries. You can even use expressions in **Visual Basic modules.**

SEE ALSO   **Functions; Validation Rules**

Favorites

Windows maintains a list of favorite web pages. Although you create this list of favorites with Windows or Microsoft Internet Explorer, the favorites list is relevant to Access. Both the Open and Save dialog boxes provide a Favorites shortcut icon you can click to display the favorites list.

Field

The columns in a **table** are called fields. Each field stores the same type of information. In an address book database, for example, you might have a street address column; so "street address" is a field.

A curious but powerful feature of Access is that it doesn't limit you to storing only text and numbers in fields. You can also store **OLE objects,** which means that you can put a picture in a **database,** for example. It also means that you can put another application's **document** in a database.

SEE ALSO   Object

Field Names

You name **fields** when you create a **table.** You can use as many as 64 characters for a field name—including all letters and numbers and most special characters. (You can't use periods, exclamation points, or brackets.) You can use blank spaces, but you can't start a field name with a blank space.

Spaces in a field name

Although you can use spaces in field names, it's better if you don't. Field names without spaces are usually easier to use in **expressions** and are easier to **export.**

Field Property

When you define a **field,** you name it and assign a **data type** to it. You can even add a description that's displayed on the status bar whenever the field is selected. (This last step really is a good idea.) You can describe a field in more detail than this, however, by using field properties.

Changing Field Properties

1 Open in Design view the table containing the fields whose properties you want to change. The bottom half contains the properties boxes.

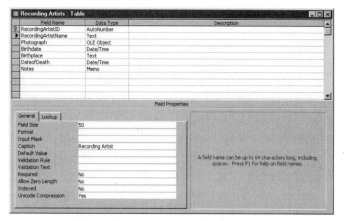

2 If the General tab isn't already selected, click it.

3 Select the field property you want to edit. Access typically adds an arrow button just to the right of the property box. You can click this arrow to see a drop-down list box of the property settings available for the selected field.

Changing the Field Size Property for a Text Field

The Text Field Size property tells Access how many characters can be inserted in a field. You simply click the Field Size box, and enter a number. A text field needs to be long enough to hold the full range of possible entries (or reasonable abbreviations). Don't make a text field longer than is necessary, however. (The maximum length for text fields is 255 characters.) Doing so makes it possible for someone to enter an incorrect, long entry.

Field size and disk space

You don't use up extra space by setting the field size to a big number. For example, if you set a field used for storing 2-character state abbreviations to 50 characters in length but enter only 2-character state abbreviations, Access stores the field contents on disk in 2-character blocks, not in 50-character blocks.

Changing the Field Size Property for Number and AutoNumber Fields

The Number And AutoNumber Field Size property tells Access the maximum size a value can be in the field. The following table lists the choices:

Field Size	Range of values field can hold
Byte	Integers from 0 to 255.
Integer	Integers from -32768 to 32767.
Long Integer	Integers from -2,147,483,648 to 2,147,483,647.
Single	Values with 7 decimal places from -3.4×10^{38} to 3.4×10^{38}.
Double	Values with 15 decimal places from -1.797×10^{308} to 1.797×10^{308}.
Replication ID	Used for globally unique identifiers, or GUIDs, so the range of values doesn't apply here.
Decimal	Controls the number of decimal places in a number.

Choose the smallest size that works

The larger the numbers that fit in a field, the more room the field occupies. The Byte field size, for example, occupies only a single byte. The Integer size occupies 2 bytes; the Long Integer and Single sizes, 4 bytes; the Double size, 8 bytes; and the Replication ID size, 16 bytes.

Changing the Format of Number, AutoNumber, and Currency Fields

If the selected field is a number, an **AutoNumber,** or a currency field, you can select the Format box and select an entry from the Format drop-down list box. Although the number formats are all self-explanatory, if you have a question, just experiment.

continues

Field Property *(continued)*

Changing the Format of a Date/Time Field

Access lets you display dates in a variety of formats.

Changing the Format of a Yes/No Field

Yes/No fields can hold any of these three sets of answers: Yes or No, True or False, or On or Off. You choose which set of answers is valid for the field by selecting the Yes/No field and then using the Format drop-down list box.

Creating an Input Mask

An input mask helps you enter information into a field in a predefined format. For example, if you want to store the telephone number *2065551234* as *(206) 555-1234*, you can create an input mask that adds the parentheses, space, and hyphen. To create an input mask for the selected field, click the Input Mask property text box and then click the button that appears just to the right of the box. This action starts the Input Mask Wizard, which steps you through the process of creating an input mask.

Specifying Decimal Places for Number and Currency Fields

You can specify how many decimal places Access should use to display a field's value by using the Decimal Places property. To use your selected format's default number of decimal places, select the Auto entry. When you've selected the General Number format, the Decimal Places property has no effect.

Adding a Caption

Access uses a caption to label input blanks—text boxes, really—on the datasheet, on the **forms** you use to collect field data, and on **reports** that summarize the data. To add a caption, fill in the Caption property box. The Caption field works the same for all data types.

Suggesting Default Text or Value Entries for Fields

You can suggest an entry for a field by filling in the Default Value property box. You can enter a block of text, a number, or an **expression** that returns a value.

If you were building a names-and-addresses table in which you thought most of the addresses would be in the United States, you might use the text *US* as the default value for the country field.

You can also specify a default value for a number field.

You can also enter a formula, or expression, that returns a value. For example, the expression =DATE() plugs the current system date into a field as the default entry. Date() is only one of the **functions** you can use in Access.

For help with building an expression, click the button to the right of the Default Value property box. This action opens the Expression Builder dialog box.

Validating Field Entries

You can also tell Access to validate field entries. You enter **validation rules** in the Validation Rule property box.

Validation Error Messages

If you specify a validation rule for a field, you can use the Validation Text property box to specify the error message Access will return if a field entry doesn't pass the validation test.

Why You Should Be Careful in Setting Field Properties

Forms and reports you create for viewing or changing data from the table inherit many of the field properties. For example, if you specify a validation rule for a field, Access uses the rule to check the data you enter in a form.

File

Programs such as Windows Explorer and Access get stored on your disk as files. The **databases** you create in Access—including all the **objects** that constitute the database—also get stored on disk as files. In general, you manipulate the location of files—even database files—with Windows Explorer, and you manipulate the contents of the database files—table **records,** for example—with Access.

Filenames

You give a **database** its filename when you create the database. (Although you create databases in a variety of ways, perhaps the most common way is by starting the **Database Wizard.**)

File-Naming Rules

Files saved in Windows don't have to observe the old 8-character MS-DOS naming rule. You can save your database files with names as long as 255 characters. All the numbers and letters that appear on the keyboard are okay, and so are many other characters. You can use spaces. You can't, however, use these characters: / ? : * " < > |. Be aware that certain programs you may use (such as file-compression and e-mail programs) may truncate long filenames.

Specifying File Extensions

The file extension, by the way, isn't something you need to worry about. Access adds the file extension MDB to identify the file as an Access database file.

SEE ALSO   Object

Filter

A filter is a set of selection criteria or sorting specifications you use to limit and organize the **records** displayed in a **form** or a **datasheet.** If you're in the process of designing a **query,** you don't need to create a filter. You can enter the selection criteria as part of designing the query.

Filtering by Selection

The easiest way to filter the records in a form or datasheet is by displaying the form or datasheet, finding a record like the one you want to filter, and then clicking the field you want to use as a filter.

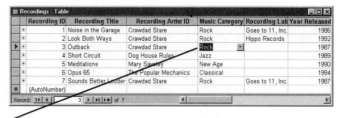

To filter a project list so that only rock recordings show, for example, select a Project Name field that shows "Rock."

When you've selected the field you'll use to filter, click the Filter By Selection toolbar button.

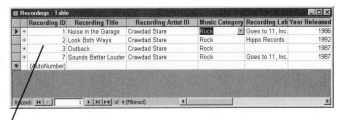

This is the filtered list of projects.

Filtering by Form

To use the Filter By Form feature, display the form or datasheet with the records you want to filter. Then click the Filter By Form toolbar button.

In the Filter By Form window, click the field you want to filter by, open its drop-down list box, and select one of the list entries that are displayed. Then click the Apply Filter toolbar button.

Using an Advanced Filter

To create an advanced filter, first display the form or the datasheet you want to filter. Choose the Records menu's Filter command and the submenu's Advanced Filter/Sort command. When Access displays the Filter Design View window, indicate the field you'll use to sort, the sort order, and any selection criteria.

Specifying fields, sort orders, and selection criteria for an advanced filter works in the same manner as specifying fields, sort orders, and selection criteria for a query.

To use a filter you've just created, choose the Records menu's Apply Filter/Sort command or click the Apply Filter toolbar button.

Unfiltering Records

To unfilter the records, choose the Records menu's Remove Filter/Sort command or click the Apply Filter toolbar button again.

Finding Records

To find a specific **record**, display either a **form** or the **datasheet** for the **table** that stores the record. Select the field you want to search, and then choose the Edit menu's Find command or click the Find toolbar button.

1 Enter the text you're looking for in the Find What text box.

2 Specify which field to search in the Look In text box. Although searching only the current field is faster, you have to make sure that the insertion point is in the field that contains the data.

Find and Replace

Find	Replace

Find What: | Garage | ▼ | Find Next |
| | | Cancel |

Look In: | Recording Title | ▼ |

Match: | Whole Field | ▼ | More >> |

3 Use the Match drop-down list box to tell Access whether what you're looking for starts the field, is somewhere within the field, or makes up the entire field.

5 Click Find Next to start and restart the search.

4 Click More for other options: whether to search the table up, down, or both ways and whether to match the case and formatting of the text you've entered. Access normally ignores both case and formatting.

Wildcards

You can use **wildcard characters** in your Find What entry. The ? character represents any single character. The * character represents any single character or combination of characters. The # character represents any single digit. The #* characters (in combination) represent any number.

Foreign Key

A foreign key is the **common field** in a related **table**. A **primary key**, in comparison, is the common field in the **primary table**.

Format Painter

Access, like the other Microsoft Office applications, now has a Format Painter toolbar button. Most Access users probably won't use it, however. Its purpose is to copy the formatting of **control objects**.

Forms

A form lets you enter, edit, and view **table** and **query** data.

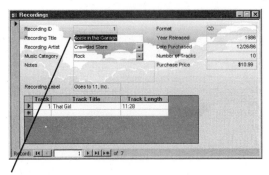

On a form, each field gets its own box or button. You can design forms that use all the elements of the Windows interface: check boxes, option buttons, and list boxes, for example.

Creating a Form with the Form Wizard

To create a form by using the Form Wizard, follow these steps:

1 Open the Database Window in the database to which the form should be added.

2 Click Forms.

3 Click New. Access displays the New Form dialog box.

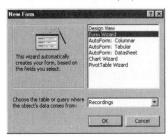

continues

Forms *(continued)*

4 Open the drop-down list box, and select the **object** on which the form will be based.

5 Select which sort of form you want to create—from scratch in Design view or with one of a half-dozen different wizards.

6 Click OK.

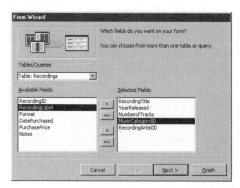

7 Select the fields you want in the order they should appear on the form. You can select individual table fields by clicking the field in the Available Fields list box and then clicking the > button. Or you can select all the table's fields by clicking the >> button. You can remove a field from the Selected Fields list box by clicking it and clicking the < button. You can remove all the fields from the Selected Fields list box by clicking the << button.

8 Click Next.

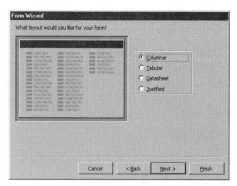

9 Choose how you want the fields arranged on your form. You can use the preview area on the left side of the dialog box to get a rough idea of how the fields will be laid out.

10 Click Next.

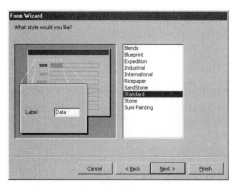

11 Select a style from the dialog box's list box. The preview area on the left side of the dialog box shows the different backgrounds available for the form.

12 Click Next.

13 Pick a name for your form. Then choose whether you want to start using the form or redesign some of the form by fiddling with its **control objects.** You can replace the suggested name if you want. You probably don't have to worry about redesigning the form, however—especially if you're in a hurry.

14 When you're done, click Finish. Access will display your new form.

continues

Forms *(continued)*

Editing Data with a Form

Access initially shows the first table record in the form. (If no records are in the table or query, the form's boxes are blank.) To find a record, you can move back and forth through the table's records by pressing the PgUp and PgDn keys. Or click the buttons on the bottom of the form. You can move back and forth through the form's fields by pressing the Tab and Shift+Tab keys.

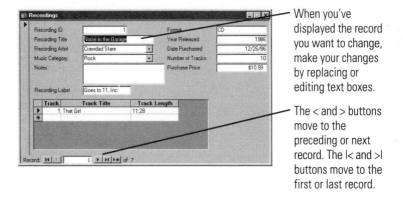

When you've displayed the record you want to change, make your changes by replacing or editing text boxes.

The < and > buttons move to the preceding or next record. The |< and >| buttons move to the first or last record.

Entering Data into a Form

To enter a new record into a table by using a form, click the >* button to display a new, empty record. Or choose the Records menu's Data Entry command. Either way, Access displays a blank form. All you do is fill in the blanks.

Making Simple Form Design Changes

You can make a number of changes to your form design. However, I'm only going to describe one change: rearranging the text boxes on the form. Display the form, and click the Design View toolbar button.

When Access displays the Design view of the form, drag the boxes around the screen by using the mouse.

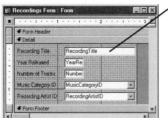

To move both the box and its description together, select either object and then drag.

Printing Forms

You can print forms for all the records in a table or a query or for only the record that's displayed.

1 Display the form. If you want to print only one record, display that record.

2 Choose the File menu's Print command.

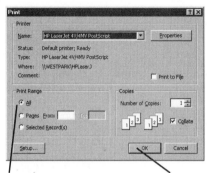

3 Click the All option button if you want to print all the records, or click the Selected Records option button if you want to print only the record you've selected.

4 Click OK.

Closing a Form

When you finish entering or editing information in a form, close the form by clicking its Close button. Or choose the File menu's Close command.

If you haven't closed the form before, Access asks whether you want to save it. Because you probably do, click Yes. Access next presents a dialog box you can use to give the form a more useful name than Form1. You can (and should) do so.

Using an Existing Form

To use a form you've already created, open the database, click the Form object tab, and then double-click the form. Access then displays the form.

SEE ALSO   **AutoForm Wizard; Graphs; Object Names; Primary Key; Printing**

Functions

Functions are prefabricated formulas you use in **expressions** and in **Visual Basic modules.** Access provides functions that perform financial, mathematical, and statistical calculations.

Functions in Access closely resemble functions in Microsoft Excel

Many functions in Access work like those in a spreadsheet. If you've used functions in Excel or in Lotus 1-2-3, you'll find using functions in Access easy and straightforward.

Graphs

Access comes with the Microsoft Graph application, which lets you easily create charts based on information shown in a **table** or a **query.** You can add graphs to **reports** and **forms,** although if you want just a quick-and-dirty chart, the easiest way to add it is to create a form by just using the Chart Wizard. To run the Chart Wizard, see the entry **Forms,** "Creating a Form with the Form Wizard," and in step 5 select Chart Wizard.

For Microsoft Excel users

In Access, the Chart Wizard—which is the wizard that creates a graph—is almost identical to the Chart Wizard in Excel. If you've created a chart in Excel, you'll find creating a graph in Access easy.

Help

Windows and almost all Windows-based applications (such as Access) include an online help feature, which means that information is almost always just a click or a keystroke away. You access this help by using one of the Help menu commands.

I'm not going to get into the intricacies of the Windows help system. If you're not familiar with how the system works, however, take the time to get to know about this handy feature.

Getting Help in Access

Need help with an Access task? Choose the Help menu's What's This? command. Access adds a question mark to the mouse pointer arrow.

Click the item you want help with. Help will display specific information about what you selected. Or click the **Office Assistant** toolbar button to ask the Office Assistant for help.

History

Access maintains a history of the databases you've used. You can view this history from either the Open or Save dialog boxes by clicking the History shortcut.

HTML

HTML stands for hypertext markup language. HTML is essentially the language the Internet uses for web pages. When your web browser displays a web page, what you're really viewing is an HTML document.

HTML is also relevant to Access, which lets you save your documents (using the HTML file format) as **data access pages,** a special type of web page. This feature enables you to post data from a database on the web so that people can access it and change it.

Hyperlink

You can put a link to basically any Internet resource—including **World Wide Web** pages—or local network resource in your worksheets by using the Insert menu's Hyperlink command.

You can create a table in which each record has its own hyperlink to a different destination. Suppose that you are a high-school guidance counselor and you want to have a table that lists all the colleges your graduating seniors might apply to. You could link each college in your table with its own web page so that students using the table could connect to the web pages of all the colleges they're interested in. Or maybe you're a manufacturer and you want to link to the web pages of all the suppliers from whom you buy parts.

continues

Hyperlink *(continued)*

To create a separate hyperlink for each record in a table, you must first create a hyperlink **field**.

Creating a Hyperlink Field in a Table

To create a hyperlink field in a table, follow these steps:

1 Either display in **Design view** the table to which you want to add the hyperlink or create a new table.

2 Click in the first blank row of the Field Name column, and give the field a name.

3 In the **Data Type** column, select Hyperlink from the drop-down list.

4 Click Save to save the table.

Inserting Hyperlinks into a Table

When you've created a table with a hyperlink field, follow these steps to forge the hyperlinks:

1 Switch to Datasheet view.

2 Click in the hyperlink field for each record, and type the display text—the actual text you want users of the table to see. (For a link to the University of Washington web page, for example, you might type *UW Web Page*.) The display text appears underlined and in blue.

3 Click the Insert Hyperlink toolbar button.

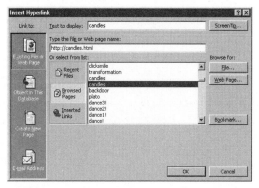

4 Use the shortcuts on the left to indicate whether you want to link to an existing file or web page, an object in the active database, a new document you create now, or an e-mail address. Enter the URL of the web page you want to link to, or select from the lists of Recent Files, Browsed Pages, or Inserted Links.

5 Click OK to add the hyperlink to the field.

When you position the mouse pointer over the new hyperlink, it changes to a hand icon. Click to open the linked web page. To edit the hyperlink, click the Insert Hyperlink toolbar button again to open the Edit Hyperlink dialog box.

Changing the appearance of hyperlinks

Hyperlinks in your tables will appear by default in underlined, blue text. After you've followed a hyperlink, it turns purple. You can change the way hyperlinks look. Just choose the Tools menu's Options command, and click the General tab. Click Web Options. Change the options under the Hyperlinks heading to make your hyperlinks appear the way you want by choosing a color from the drop-down list.

SEE ALSO Field Property; HTML

Importing Data

You can import data stored in a table file that is external to Access by either linking the **table** with the data to an existing **database** or actually importing the file into Access. (When you link a table, the data stays in the other, external file. When you import the file, it becomes a table **object** in an Access database file.)

Linking an External Table

To link an external table to the open Access database:

1 Choose the File menu's Get External Data command and the submenu's Link Tables command. Access displays the Link dialog box.

continues

Importing Data *(continued)*

2 Identify the file, and specify its location; then click Link. (This dialog box works like the one you use to open a database file.) Access displays the Link Tables dialog box.

3 Select the table, and click OK.

Importing a Table

To import a table into Access, follow these steps:

1 Choose the File menu's Get External Data command and the submenu's Import command. Access displays the Import dialog box.

2 Identify the file, and specify its location; then click Import. (This dialog box works like the one you use to open a database file.)

3 When Access displays the Import Objects dialog box, select the table and click OK.

Importing Other Database Objects

The Import Objects dialog box lets you import database objects other than tables. You import these other database objects in the same way you import tables.

Which database files you can import

Which database files you can import depends on which database drivers you installed as part of setting up Access.

Index

A database index works in a manner similar to a library card catalog. Whether it's on paper cards or a computer, a library card catalog provides a list of the books in the library and their locations. By looking through the card catalog, you save yourself the trouble (and the time) of having to search every shelf in every bookcase on every floor of the library.

In the same manner, a database index provides a list of the **records** in a **table** and their disk location. An index makes **querying** a database much faster because Access has to search only the index (which resides mostly in memory) rather than each of the individual records (which reside on your disk).

If you've created a **primary key** for a table, it becomes the index. If you haven't created a primary key, Access asks whether it can add an index when you save the table. If you answer Yes, it does, calling the index something like "ID."

Adding a Single-Field Index

To add a single-field index to a table, follow these steps:

1 Open the **Database Window.**

2 Click Table.

3 Select the table, and click Design. Access displays the Design View window for the table object.

4 Select the **field** you want to use for the index.

5 Click in the Indexed **field property** box.

6 Open the Indexed drop-down list box, and select either the Yes (No Duplicates) or Yes (Duplicates OK) entry.

continues

Index *(continued)*

Removing an Index

If you make a mistake in assigning an index, you can remove it:

1 Open the Database Window.

2 Click Table.

3 Select the table, and click Design. Access displays the Design View window for the table object.

4 Select the Index field.

5 Click in the Indexed field property box.

6 Open the Indexed drop-down list box, and click No.

Adding a Multiple-Field Index

You can add a multiple-field index to a table too. You might do this if you frequently sort based on several fields. By creating a multiple-field index, you increase the speed of the sort operation.

1 Open the Database Window.

2 Click Table.

3 Select the table, and click Design. Access displays the Design View window for the table object.

4 Click the Indexes toolbar button.

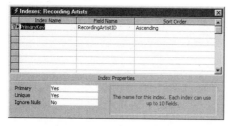

5 Select the first blank row.

6 Label the index in the Index Name column.

7 Use the Field Name column to enter the field names that should constitute the index in the order in which they should be used to sort: primary key, secondary key, tertiary key, and so on. Separate the field names by entering them in different rows.

8 Click the Close button.

9 Close the Design View window for the table object. When Access asks whether you want to save your changes, click Yes.

Installing Access

Microsoft Office 2000 is very smart about the way it installs Access and the other Office programs on your computer. For example, the Office setup program looks at your computer and any previous installations before it installs Access, in order to install only the parts of Access you're likely to use. If some piece of the Access program becomes damaged or necessary, Access will automatically repair itself by reinstalling damaged components or installing missing components. For these reasons, you may occasionally be prompted to supply the Office or Access CD.

Joining Tables

When you want to combine two or more **tables** in a single **query**, Access "joins" them. Join is a database buzzword, so you can think about joins as combinations.

If you've defined a **relationship** between the two tables, Access already knows how to join, or combine, them. When you add both tables to the query, Access draws a join line between the table's **common fields.** (Because it's the best way to proceed, you might flip to the **Relationships** entry to see how this relationship-building business works.)

If you haven't defined a relationship, you can tell Access how it should join the tables as part of setting up the query. Select the common field in the **primary table**—for example, by clicking it—and then drag it to the common field in the related table. To delete a join, select the join line that Access adds and then press the Delete key.

Joining tables that don't share a common field

You can join tables that don't share a common field by including a third table that has common fields for the other two tables. In this case, you might be able to connect table 1 to table 2 with one common field and then connect table 2 to table 3 with another common field. When you're finished, you can combine, or join, table 1 and table 3 in a query.

SEE ALSO Equi-Join; Outer-Join; Self-Join

Keyboard Navigation

You can use the keyboard to move through the **records** in a **table,** through the **fields** in a record, and through the characters in a field text box. The following table lists keyboard navigation techniques:

Key	What it does
Up	Moves selection cursor to preceding record in a datasheet or to the preceding field in a form.
Down	Moves selection cursor to the next record in a datasheet or to the next field in a form.
Left	Moves insertion point one character to the left.
Right	Moves insertion point one character to the right.
Ctrl+Up	Moves selection cursor to top of column or to the same field in the first record shown in a datasheet.
Ctrl+Down	Moves selection cursor to bottom of column or to the same field in the last record shown in a datasheet.
Ctrl+Left	Moves insertion point one word left.
Ctrl+Right	Moves insertion point one word right.
Tab	Moves selection cursor to the next field.
Shift+Tab	Moves selection cursor to the preceding field.
Enter	Moves selection cursor to the next field.
Ctrl+Enter	Ends a line of text in a Memo field.
PgUp	Scrolls up what's shown in the window.
PgDn	Scrolls down what's shown in the window.
Ctrl+PgUp	Scrolls left what's shown in the window.
Ctrl+PgDn	Scrolls right what's shown in the window.
Home	Moves selection cursor to the first field in a record.
End	Moves selection cursor to the last field in a record.
Ctrl+Home	Moves selection cursor to the first field in a table.
Ctrl+End	Moves selection cursor to the last field in a table.

Changing the default key assignment

By the way, if you don't agree with these commands, you can change some of them. Choose the Tools menu's Options command, and click the Keyboard tab.

Differentiating the Insertion Point and the Selection Cursor

The insertion point is the vertical bar that shows the placement of what you type. If you can't figure out the placement, start a Windows-based application such as WordPad, begin typing, and look at the bar that moves ahead of the text you type. See it? That's the insertion point.

The selection cursor marks the selected option in a dialog box or the selected text in a box or the selected row in a datasheet. The way Windows marks objects with the selection cursor depends on the object being marked.

Navigating with the mouse

You can move around a table, a form, or a text box by clicking what you want to select.

Laptop Computers

If you're using Access on a laptop computer, you should know that almost everything described in this book still applies. You should also consider two other, minor points. First, because pointing devices on a laptop are often challenging to use, remember that everything you want to do can also be accomplished with your keyboard. You can select the menu bar, for example, by pressing the Alt key. After you've done that, you can select menus and commands by pressing the underlined letter or number in their name.

A second point to remember is that some of the Access installation features won't work on your laptop unless you have access to the original Access installation information—such as the original installation CD. As described in the **Installing Access** and **Detect And Repair** entries, Access may need to install additional components of the program as you work or may need to repair damaged components of the program.

Logical Operators

You can use logical operators to construct logical **expressions** for **validation rules** and to construct selection criteria for **queries.** The following table describes and illustrates the most common of these powerful features:

Operator	Description and example
=	Equals. If you enter the logical expression =*100* as a validation rule for the Deposit field, you've said that a deposit must equal 100.
>	Greater than. If you enter the logical expression >*100* as a validation rule for the Deposit field, you've said that a deposit must be greater than 100.
<	Less than. If you enter the logical expression <*100* as a validation rule for the Deposit field, you've said that a deposit must be less than 100.
>=	Greater than or equal to. If you enter the logical expression >=*100* as validation rule for the Deposit field, you've said that a deposit must be greater than or equal to 100.
<=	Less than or equal to. If you enter the logical expression <=*100* as a validation rule for the Deposit field, you've said that a deposit must be less than or equal to 100.
<>	Not equal to. If you enter the logical expression <>*100* as a validation rule for the Deposit field, you've said that a deposit must not equal 100.
And	This operator combines expressions. For the combined expression to be true, each of the component expressions must be true. If you enter the logical expression >*100 And* < *500* as a validation rule for the Deposit field, you've said that a deposit must be greater than 100 and less than 500. (In other words, the deposit must fall within the range of 100 to 500.)
Or	This operator combines expressions. For the combined expression to be true, any one of the component expressions must be true. If you enter the logical expression <*100 Or* > *500* as a validation rule for the Deposit field, you've said that a deposit must be either less than 100 or greater than 500.

Operator	Description and example
Not	This operator negates an expression. If you enter the logical expression *Not <100* as a validation rule for the Deposit field, you've said that a deposit must not be less than 100.
Between	This operator tests whether a value falls within a range. If you enter the logical expression *Between 100 And 500* as a validation rule for the Deposit field, you've said that a deposit must equal or exceed 100 but can't exceed 500.
In	This operator tests whether an entry is an item in a set. If you enter the logical expression *In (50, 100, 200)* as a validation rule for the Deposit field, you've said that a deposit must equal 50 or 100 or 200.
Is Null	This expression tests whether a field is empty. You wouldn't use this operator as a validation rule. You might use it as a selection criterion to find records with an empty Deposit field.
Is Not Null	This expression ensures that a field is not left empty. You might use it to find records with something entered in the Deposit field.
Like	This expression tests whether the entry in a text field matches a pattern. If you enter the logical expression *Like ??* as a validation rule for a State field, you've said that the State must equal two characters. If you know the State field entry should start with the letter *C,* you would enter the expression as *Like C?.*

Lookup Wizard

If you know what all the possible entries for a **field** are, you can provide this list of entries to database users wherever they enter data into or edit the data in a field. For example, if you operate a business that sells its products in only the United States, only 50 possible entries exist for a State field because only 50 states are in the United States. Rather than make database users enter a two-letter state abbreviation, then, you could provide a list box from which database users could select a two-letter state abbreviation.

continues

Lookup Wizard *(continued)*

Creating a Lookup Field

To create a Lookup field, you specify the **data type** as Lookup Wizard when you're designing the table. (You would do this by using the Design **view** of the table.) Access displays a dialog box that asks where you want to get your lookup list of entries: from another table or query or from a list you'll enter by typing. After you make your decision, click Next.

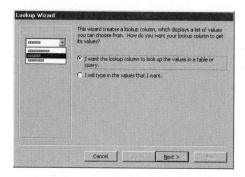

1 If you indicate that you want to get the list of entries from another table or query, the Lookup Wizard displays additional dialog boxes that ask you to identify the table or query and the field.

2 If you indicate that you want to get the list of entries by typing, the Lookup Wizard displays an additional dialog box that asks you to enter the list.

Using a Lookup Field

After you've used the Lookup Wizard to create the Lookup field, it's a snap to use the field. Access creates a combo box on **forms** and **datasheets** that show the field. To use the combo box, you either enter a new value or open the drop-down list box and select a value.

Customizing a Lookup Field

If you open a table's Design View window, you'll notice that it has, in addition to the General tab of **field properties,** a Lookup tab of field properties.

Macro Buttons

A macro button is a **control object** you can add to a **form** to automate some repetitive task related to using the form.

Creating a Macro Button

To create a macro button, follow these steps:

1 Display the form to which the macro button should be added.

2 Click Design View. Access displays the Design view of the **object** and the **toolbox.** (If Access doesn't display the toolbox, choose the View menu's Toolbox command.)

3 Click Control Wizards in the toolbox, if it isn't already selected.

4 Click the Command Button tool.

5 Place and size the command button on the form by clicking where you want to place the top left corner and then dragging the mouse to where you want to place the bottom right corner. Release the mouse button.

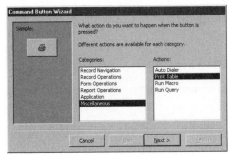

6 Select entries from the Categories and Actions list boxes to indicate what you want Access to do when you click the command button. As you select different categories, different actions are listed in the Actions list box.

7 Click Next.

continues

Macro Buttons *(continued)*

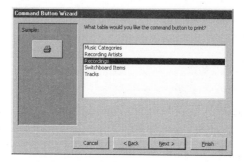

8 Provide Access with the additional information it needs to complete the action you identified in step 6. For example, if you said that you wanted Access to print a form when you click the command button, Access asks, "What form would you like the command button to print?" If the command in step 6 is simple, such as "Find Next," the wizard may skip this step.

9 Click Next.

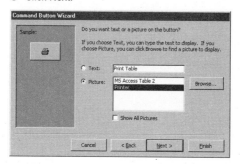

10 Describe how the button should look. You can provide a text label for the command button or specify that a picture (such as a picture of a printer) be used.

11 Click Next.

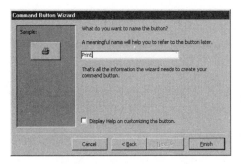

12 Name the command button control object, preferably a name that tells you what the button does. By the way, if you write **Visual Basic modules** that act on control objects, you would use the name you assign in this step.

13 Click Finish. Access adds the command button to the form.

14 Choose the File menu's Save command to save the form design changes. Or close the Form Design View window, and Access will prompt you to save changes.

Macros

A macro is simply a list of commands. Access lets you store these lists and repeat, or play back, the stored commands. With this playback ability, you can automate operations that work the same way every time they are performed. Macros in Access are created by using the Visual Basic Editor command, which appears on the submenu that's displayed when you choose the Tools menu's Macro command. **Visual Basic** is beyond the scope of this book.

SEE ALSO   Macro Buttons

Mailing Labels

If you've stored names and addresses in a **table** or created a **query** that produces a names-and-addresses **dynaset,** you can easily create mailing labels. (Mailing labels, by the way, are a type of **report.**)

continues

Mailing Labels *(continued)*

Creating a Mailing Labels Report

1 Open the **Database Window** for the **database** to which the report should be added.

2 Click Reports.

3 Click New.

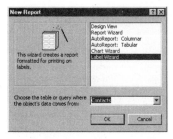

4 Select the Label Wizard entry from the list box.

5 Open the drop-down list box, and select the table or query that holds the mailing list information—names and street addresses, for example.

6 Click OK. Access asks what size mailing label you're using.

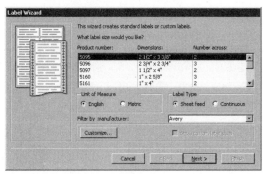

7 Select the size you're using.

8 Click Next. Access asks for your font and color choices.

9 Choose the font and color you want for the labels by using the boxes and buttons provided.

10 Click Next. Access asks which fields should appear on the label.

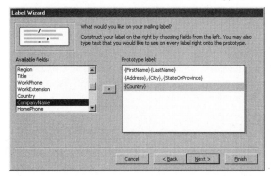

11 Select the **field** you want to appear on the first line of the mailing label, and then click the > button. (To remove a field, select it and press Delete.)

12 If you want a space or some punctuation to follow the field you just added, type the punctuation character by using the keyboard.

13 If you want the next field to appear on the next line, press Enter.

14 Repeat steps 11, 12, and 13 to add additional fields, punctuation, and spacing to the mailing label.

15 Click Next. Access asks how you want your mailing labels sorted.

continues

Mailing Labels *(continued)*

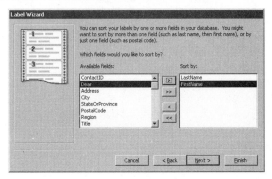

16 Select the first field you want Access to use for alphabetizing or arranging fields by clicking it and then clicking the > button. If necessary, select another field to alphabetize or arrange table records that have the same first field. You can remove a field from the Sort By list box by clicking it and clicking the < button. If you want to start over, remove all the fields from the Sort By list box by clicking the << button.

17 Click Next. Access asks whether you want to see how your mailing labels look or whether you want to modify the design. You can also choose to replace the suggested report name. Make your choices, and then click Finish.

Printing Mailing Labels

1 Preview the mailing labels report in the Print Preview window by displaying the Database Window, clicking Reports, selecting the mailing labels report, and then clicking Preview.

2 Choose the File menu's Print command. Access displays the Print dialog box.

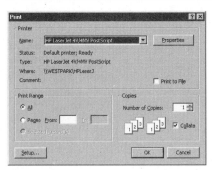

3 Complete the Print dialog box as needed.

Closing a Mailing Labels Report

When you finish reviewing the information in a mailing labels list or report, close the report by clicking its Close button. Or choose the File menu's Close command.

Using an Existing Mailing Labels List

To use a mailing labels list you've already created, display the Database Window, click Reports, and double-click the mailing labels list or click Preview. Access displays the mailing labels list in a Print Preview window.

Main Form SEE Subform

Mathematical Operators

You can use seven mathematical **operators** to build **calculated field** formulas in Access:

Operator	What it does
+	Adds values. For example, the expression 2+2 returns the not-surprising result of 4.
-	Subtracts one value from another. For example, the expression 10-2 returns 8.
*	Multiplies values. The expression 2*3 returns 6.
/	Divides values. The expression 10/3, for example, returns 3.333. (How many decimal places those 3s extend depends on the Number field's format, which determines its decimal precision.)
\	Divides values and returns the integer portion of the dividend. The expression 10\3, for example, returns 3.
^	Raises a value to a specified power. The expression 10^3 raises 10 to the third power, returning 1000.
&	Concatenates strings of text. For example, the expression *Walla&Walla* returns WallaWalla. Strictly speaking, the & operator is not mathematical.

continues

Mathematical Operators *(continued)*

Operator precedence

Access applies the standard rules of operator precedence in a formula that uses more than one operator: exponential operations are performed first, then division and multiplication, and then addition and subtraction. You can override these standard rules by using parentheses; Access will first perform operations inside parentheses.

SEE ALSO   Expressions; Query; Validation Rules

Modules

A module, another type of database **object,** is a **Visual Basic** program. To create your own modules, therefore, you need to know how to program in Visual Basic. Note, however, that nonprogrammers can create simple **macro buttons** that let them automate repetitive tasks.

My Documents

Windows supplies a folder called My Documents that Access assumes you use to store many of the documents you create. Based on this assumption, the Access Open and Save dialog boxes both provide a My Documents shortcut to quickly open the My Documents folder.

Normalization

A database designer performs normalization when he or she organizes **fields** into **tables.** Normalizing a database means eliminating repetitive fields within a table and minimizing data redundancy across the tables in the **database.**

Suppose that you build a database of students and their test scores. Rather than have one table with a lot of test score fields in it—this is repetition—you would create a test scores table in which each test and test score is inserted into its own **record,** or row. Rather than store, for example, the student's full name and address in a lot of different tables—this is data redundancy—you would store the student's name and address in only one place. (You would probably store student names and addresses in a names-and-addresses table.)

Fixing data repetition and data redundancy problems

If you have a database with lots of repetition and redundancy, Access can help you fix it. Choose the Tools menu's Analyze Tables command. Access starts a **wizard** that explains why you want to normalize the tables in your database and then splits up your tables to normalize them. (If you know how you want to split the tables, you can specify how they should be split rather than having Access do it for you.)

Object

The word *object* is an imprecise and extremely confusing term when you're talking about databases. The problem is that the word *object* refers to three different items.

Database Objects

The **tables, queries, forms, reports, macros,** and **modules** that make up a database, for example, are all objects. In other words, the major building blocks of an Access database are called objects. (I'll always call these objects "database objects.")

Control Objects

The elements Access places in a form or a report—portions of text, numbers, or calculated amounts, for example—are called objects too. I won't talk much about **control objects,** except for **macro buttons,** because you can use the **Control Wizard** feature to place and position control objects in a form or a report. (I'll always call these objects "control objects.")

continues

Object *(continued)*

OLE Objects

A third type of object in Access is an embedded or linked object. You can use these objects to create what's called a compound document.

SEE ALSO   OLE Objects

Object Buttons

Object buttons are the elements that run along the left edge of the **Database Window.** You click an object button to display a list of the database objects in that category.

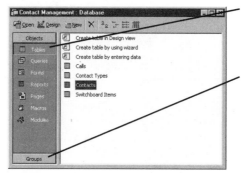

Click the Tables icon, for example, to display a list of the table objects in the database.

Access also allows you to display objects, such as Favorites, in Groups.

Object Names

Access lets you name its database **objects.** To name the active **database** object—the object in the active **document window**—choose the File menu's Save As command. Then when Access displays the Save As dialog box, enter a name. The object name should be unique. (Remember that this name will be displayed in the **Database Window** whenever the database object's **object button** is selected.)

In naming an object—such as a table, a report, or a query—Access lets you use as many as 64 characters. Although you can use spaces, you can't begin the name with a space. An object name can't contain a period, an exclamation point, brackets, or ASCII control characters.

ODBC

ODBC stands for open database connectivity. The term usually refers to drivers—little control programs—that come with Access. These ODBC drivers let you connect Access to external **SQL** databases such as Microsoft SQL Server. You choose which ODBC drivers get installed when you set up Access.

Office Assistant

Microsoft Access Help is now supplied by the Office Assistant, an animated character that pops up whenever you click the Help toolbar button or choose the Help menu's Microsoft Access Help command. When the Assistant appears, type a question and click Search. The Assistant will display the help topics that most closely relate to your question. Or click Tips, and the Assistant will display a series of tips that help you get the most from Access.

You can customize the Office assistant to suit your preferences by using the Office Assistant dialog box.

Choosing an Assistant

To pick the particular Assistant you like, right-click the Assistant and click the shortcut menu's Choose Assistant command. You can choose an Assistant from a gallery of available characters on the Gallery tab of the Office Assistant dialog box. Your choices range from a robot to a friendly dog to an Albert Einstein look-alike.

continues

Office Assistant *(continued)*

Setting Assistant Options

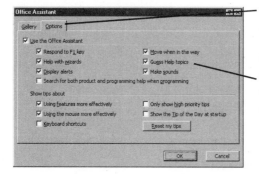

Click the Options tab to select a variety of options relating to the Assistant's capabilities.

You can also select options that control how tips are displayed.

Hiding the Assistant

If the Assistant starts to drive you crazy, you can make it go away until you need it. Right-click the Assistant, and choose the Hide command.

Office Server Extensions

The newest version of Access works with Office Server Extensions. Office Server Extensions, and a related feature called WebPost, let you save and retrieve Office documents to and from a web server. Note, however, that Office Server Extensions should be transparent to Access users and aren't something users need to work with directly. Office Server Extensions run on the web server and typically are monitored and maintained by the network or web server administrator.

OLE Objects

You can use OLE objects to create a compound document—a document file that combines two or more types of information. For example, you might want to create a compound document that includes a long report written in Microsoft Word or WordPerfect. On page 27 of your report, however, you might want to include a query created in Access. On page 37 of your report, you might want to include a chart created in Excel. Your compound document therefore consists of pieces of information—called objects—created in different programs and pasted together into one big compound document.

Creating Compound Documents

To do all this pasting and combining, you can use the program's Copy and Paste (or Paste Special) commands on the Edit menu. If you're creating the compound document in Access, you can use the Insert menu's Object command.

Distinguishing Between Linked Objects and Embedded Objects

A linked object—such as an Access query—gets updated whenever the source document changes. An embedded object doesn't. (You can, however, double-click an embedded object to open the application that created the embedded object to make your changes.)

Let me also make a somewhat obvious point. If you embed, or copy, an object into a compound document, it gets bigger. When you simply link an object, the compound document doesn't really get bigger.

What you absolutely need to know about embedded and linked objects

Perhaps the most important tidbit for you to know about objects is that they're very easy to use. You don't have to do anything other than copy and paste the objects you want to insert in the compound document.

SEE ALSO Embedding and Linking Objects

Opening Databases

To open a previously saved database, choose the File menu's Open command or click the Open toolbar button. Either way, Access displays the Open dialog box, shown here.

1 Click the **History, My Documents, Desktop, Favorites,** or **Web Folders** shortcut icon to specify where the database is located if you've previously saved, opened, or viewed the file; stored it in the My Documents folder; stored it on your desktop; added it to your Favorites folder; or retrieved it from a web folder. Alternatively, use the Look In boxes to specify where the file was saved.

2 If necessary, select a file type from the Files Of Type list box if you want to open a file with a format other than that of the usual Access database file. (You might do this if you want to import another database program's file.)

3 When you see the database file in the file list box, double-click it to open it. Alternatively, enter the database's name in the File Name box, and click Open.

Protecting the original database

If you don't want to overwrite the original database file, click the down arrow at the right end of the Open button and then choose the menu's Open Read Only command. If you choose Open Read Only and later want to save the database, you'll have to use a new filename.

SEE ALSO **Saving Databases and Objects; Troubleshooting: You Can't Find a File**

Operators

Access provides mathematical and logical operators you can use in expressions for validation rules, for selection criteria, and for calculated fields.

Calculating values and concatenating text SEE **Mathematical Operators**	
Comparing values and text SEE **Logical Operators**	

Outer-Join

When Access joins tables in a multiple-table **query,** it typically runs an **equi-join.** It means that you won't see query results unless Access can successfully join **records** in all the tables. For example, if you're joining customer table records and customer order table records, Access won't show customer order records for customers not listed in the customer table, which is usually what you want. If you don't care whether Access can successfully join records in all the tables, you can run an outer-join.

To create an outer-join, display the Query Design **View** window for the query and double-click the join line. Or click the join line, and then choose the View menu's Join Properties command.

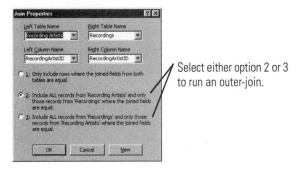

Select either option 2 or 3 to run an outer-join.

SEE ALSO   Joining Tables; Self-Join

Passwords

You can limit access to a database by adding a password. Be fore-warned, however: this procedure is much more involved than you might guess if you're used to the way passwords work in applications such as Lotus 1-2-3 or WordPerfect. In Access, passwords are only one element of a rather sophisticated security system.

To assign passwords or use other elements of the Access security system—for example, groups, user accounts, and permissions—refer to the user documentation.

Pathname

A pathname describes the location of a file on your computer or, if you're working on a local area network, on the network. Microsoft Office programs such as Access let you use pathnames when you're **opening databases** and **saving databases**—you simply enter the pathname in the File Name box.

A pathname typically consists of three parts: the disk drive letter, the folder name, and the filename. If a file named letters.htm is stored in a folder named correspondence and this folder is located on the C disk drive, the pathname is

c:\correspondence\letters.htm

Note that the disk drive letter is separated from the folder name by a colon and a backslash and that the folder name is separated from the filename by a backslash. Note also that if a file is located in a subfolder, the subfolder or subfolders become part of the pathname, too. For example, if a file named letters.htm is stored in a subfolder named January, which is stored in a folder named cor-respondence which is located on the C disk drive, the pathname is

c:\correspondence\january\letters.htm

Performance Analyzer

Building your own database can be tricky for a lot of different reasons. One tricky area is performance. Many of the little decisions you make (for example, deciding whether a **table** should have an **index** or whether a field should be text or an integer) can have a big impact on the speed with which you do tasks in your **database**.

To help you figure all this out, Access has a Performance Analyzer. It looks at a database you've built and identifies quirky design decisions—errors, really—that will cause performance problems in your database. Performance Analyzer can fix your design errors in some cases. In other cases, it can simply suggest a change that, if you want, you can make on your own.

To use Performance Analyzer, follow these steps:

1 Choose the Tools menu's Analyze command and the submenu's Performance command.

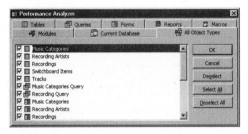

2 Click one of the tabs in the dialog box to select an object type. If you want to analyze all the objects in your database, click the All Object Types tab.

3 Identify the database objects you want to analyze. Select the check boxes for the objects you want Access to analyze. If you want Access to analyze all the objects—and you probably do—click Select All.

4 Click OK. Access begins analyzing the objects you specified. A few minutes later, it displays a dialog box that lists fixes it has made and any recommendations, suggestions, and ideas it has.

continues

Performance Analyzer *(continued)*

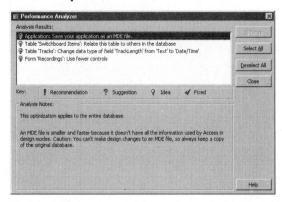

5 Select which recommendations or suggestions you want to implement by individually clicking them. (You can't use Performance Analyzer to implement ideas—only to make recommendations and suggestions.)

6 Click Optimize to follow through on the recommendations or suggestions you selected. Access may prompt you for more information as it makes the performance enhancements. For example, if it suggests that you add a new form, you'll have to give the new form a name.

Personal Menus and Toolbars

Access 2000 automatically customizes its menus by hiding commands you don't use and displaying those you do use. Usually, this **adaptability** feature enhances your use of Access because menus are less cluttered. But if you don't find personalized menus helpful, you can override the way Access makes these changes by choosing the Tools menu's Options command and then clearing the Menus Show Recently Used Commands First check box.

Access also lets you customize its toolbars and combine multiple toolbars into a single new Personal toolbar that is displayed beneath the menu bar. To create a Personal toolbar, drag a toolbar onto the same line as an existing toolbar.

Primary Key

The primary key is a **field** or a combination of fields that uniquely identifies each **record** in a **table**. The primary key is also the **common field** in a **primary table**. Although you don't have to create primary keys for tables, it's a good idea to do so. Primary keys improve performance and make defining **relationships** easier.

You create a primary key as you design or redesign a table. Select the field you want to use as the primary key, and then choose the Edit menu's Primary Key command or click the Primary Key toolbar button.

SEE ALSO Foreign Key; Index

Primary Table

A primary table in this Pocket Guide is called the main, or dominant, **table** in a table **relationship**. For example, in a database that holds customer information and customer orders information, your primary table will be the table that describes your customers. (The other table, the related table, will be the one that describes your customer orders.)

Although the issue of primary tables vs. related tables sounds somewhat odd at first, let me make three observations that may help to clear up any confusion. The primary table in a relationship will probably be the one that you fill first. In the case of a customer-and-order database, for example, someone probably becomes a customer before or while you fill a customer order—not after.

The relationship between a primary table and a related table is often (although not always) a "one-to-many" relationship. In the case of a customer-and-orders database, *one* customer table record will probably tie to *many* customer order table records. (Other books call the primary table the "one" table for this reason.)

continues

Primary Table *(continued)*

Finally, a primary table often contains information you use and would have to duplicate repeatedly in the related table. For example, if you put both customer and order information in the same table, you would enter much of the same customer information every time you processed an order: the customer name, the address, and the shipping method, for example.

You can have more than one primary table in a database

Each table relationship has a primary table. If you have more than one table relationship in a database, therefore, you'll have more than one primary table. In fact, a table might possibly be a related table in one relationship and a primary table in another relationship.

SEE ALSO Primary Key

Printing

When you tell a program such as Access to print a **document**—perhaps a **dynaset**, a **form**, or a **report**—what really happens is that the program creates a printable copy of the document called a spool file and sends it to Windows. Windows then prints the document.

SEE ALSO Mailing Labels

Program

Programs are software tools you use to do work—such as word processing, spreadsheets, database work, accounting, and many other tasks.

Microsoft sells several well-known and very popular programs, including Access (the database program this book describes), Microsoft Excel (a spreadsheet program), and Microsoft Word (a word processor). Lots of other popular and well-known applications are available too: WordPerfect, Lotus 1-2-3, and Quicken, to name a few.

Program Errors

Sometimes a **program**—Access or another application—asks Windows to do the impossible. When this happens, Windows displays a message box that alerts you to a program, or application, error.

SEE ALSO **Troubleshooting: You Get an Application Error**

Program Window

The program window is the rectangle in which a **program,** or application, such as Access displays its menu bar, toolbars, and open **document windows.**

Property

A property is simply a characteristic of a **database** object and of elements that constitute a database object. You can change the **field properties** of the **fields** in a **table,** for example. (A table is one example of a database object.)

Query

A query is fundamentally a question you ask Access about data in a **table,** in a set of tables, or in another query. Suppose that you've created a customer **database.** You might ask, "Who are my customers?" or "How many customers do I have?" Both questions are, in the parlance of databases, queries.

To query a database, you create a new database query object by doing three things: tell Access which tables or queries you want to query (you can query queries); tell it which **fields** you want it to return as part of the answer; and describe any manipulation—sorting or selection, for example—that should be performed as part of the query.

continues

Query *(continued)*

Identifying the Database and Tables

To identify the database and tables, follow these steps:

1 Open the database to which the query should be added and display the **Database Window.**

2 Click Queries.

3 Click New. Access displays the New Query dialog box.

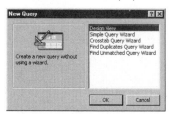

4 Assuming that you're not interested in creating a **crosstab** query or one of the other special queries listed, select Design View and click OK. Access opens the Query Design View window and displays the Show Table dialog box.

5 Select the table you'll query by clicking it and then clicking Add.

6 Repeat step 5 for each table you want to query. You can also query queries: if the data you want to ask a question about is itself in a query, click the Queries tab and then select the query.

7 Close the Show Table dialog box by clicking Close. Access displays the Query Design View window with boxes representing each of the to-be-queried tables or queries.

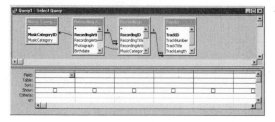

Joining Tables

If you want to combine, or **join,** tables in a query, the tables must be connected by a **common field,** and you have to identify this common field by either setting up a **relationship** or dragging the common field from the **primary table** to the common field in the related table. For example, if you're querying both a customer table and projects table and both tables have the field Customer ID, you have a common field you can use to connect the tables. Access identifies a join by drawing a line between the common fields.

Choosing the Information the Query Returns

After you identify the tables you'll query, you tell Access which fields you want the query results to show by using the **query design grid.** To do this, follow these steps:

1 Select the leftmost Field text box, and open its drop-down list box. (The drop-down list box arrow won't show until you select the field.)

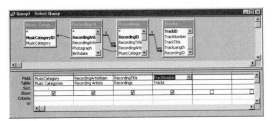

2 Select the first field that you want to see in the query results **dynaset,** that you want to use to sort, or that you want to use to select records. If you're querying multiple tables, Access identifies both the table and the field names. (You can also select fields by dragging them down from the tables to the grid.)

3 Repeat step 2 for each field you want.

You can move and remove query fields

You can move a field and its column to a new location by selecting it and then dragging it to a new location. You can remove a field from the query by selecting it and then pressing Delete or choosing the Edit menu's Delete command.

continues

Query *(continued)*

Running the Query

To run the query after you've told Access what you want to see, choose the View menu's Datasheet command or click the Run toolbar button.

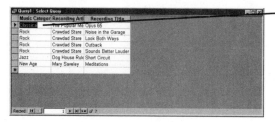

This data sheet shows the results of the query that lists the current unit price for each product.

Sorting the Query Results

To tell Access how it should sort the query results, follow these steps:

1 In Design **view**, select the field that Access should use first to alphabetize or order the query results dynaset. For example, if you're querying an Access customer database, perhaps about year-to-date orders, you might want to alphabetize the query results by customer name.

2 Open the Sort drop-down list box for the field.

3 Select the sort order you want: Ascending, Descending, or not sorted.

4 To use another field to sort query results that have the same first, or primary, sort field, repeat steps 1 through 3.

Another Way to Sort Query Results

In Datasheet view, select the column with the field you want to sort. Choose the Records menu's Sort command and the submenu's Sort Ascending or Sort Descending command. Or you can right-click the field and choose the shortcut menu's Sort Ascending or Sort Descending command. Or click the Sort Ascending or Sort Descending toolbar buttons.

The trick to multiple-key sorting

The only trick to using a second key for sorting records with the same first key is that the secondary sort key must be in a column to the right of the first sort key. Similarly, if you want to use a third sort key for records with the same first and second sort keys, the third sort key must be in a column to the right of the second sort key's column.

Specifying Selection Criteria for the Query

Use the Criteria and Or fields to specify whether you want the query to include or exclude information based on the contents of a field.

1 In Design **view**, select the field that Access should use first to select information for the query. If you're querying an Access customer database, perhaps about year-to-date international orders, you might want to exclude orders from domestic customers.

2 Enter the selection criteria for a field in the field's column. If you want to find records with a field equal to a specific value, enter that value. If you want to find records with a text field holding a specific entry—such as the state equal to CA—enter that text. You can use **logical operators** to describe selection criteria.

Compound selection criteria

If you want to search for records with fields that meet all the selection criteria listed, enter the selection criteria into the same row of the query design grid. If you want to search for records with fields that meet any one of the selection criteria, enter the selection criteria into separate rows of the query design grid.

Example Number-Field Selection Criteria

It isn't difficult to enter selection criteria into the Query Design View window after you get the hang of it, although it can be a little tricky at first. The following table shows examples of number-field selection criteria:

Criterion	What it finds
5000	Finds records in which the field entry equals 5000.
>5000	Finds records in which the field entry is greater than 5000.
>5000 And <10000	Finds records in which the field entry is greater than 5000 and less than 10000.
>=[Sales]*.75	Finds records in which the field entry is greater than or equal to 0.75, or 75 percent, of the value in the field named Sales. Entering this criterion for the field Cost of Goods, for example, finds records in which the Cost of Goods value is greater than or equal to 75 percent of the Sales value.
<1/1/95	Finds records in which the date field entry falls before January 1, 1995 (assuming that this is the criterion for a Date/Time field).

continues

Query *(continued)*

Example Text-Field Selection Criteria

Text selection criteria work differently. You can enclose the text in quotation marks. If you don't include the quotation marks, however, Access adds them for you. I've shown criteria that result in the same query results, by the way, to illustrate that you often have more than one way to accomplish the same thing. The following table shows examples of text-field selection criteria:

Criterion	What it finds
WA	Finds records in which the field entry is *WA*.
"WA"	Finds records in which the field entry is *WA*.
="WA"	Finds records in which the field entry is *WA*.
W?	Finds records in which the field entry is two characters and starts with the letter *W*.
Like ("W?")	Finds records in which the field entry matches this pattern: a two-character entry that starts with the letter *W*.
W*	Finds records in which the field entry starts with the letter *W*. The field entry can be any length.
WA	Finds records in which the field entry uses the two-letter combination *WA* anywhere within it.

Searching for embedded text in Memo and OLE object fields

You can use the asterisk character at the beginning and end of embedded text fragments you want to search for in Memo fields and in embedded (but not linked) OLE object fields.

Summary Calculations in a Query

To summarize the results of a query, construct the query in the usual way and click the Totals toolbar button so that Access adds the Total row to the query design grid. Then open the Group By drop-down list box, and select the summary calculation you want Access to make for a field.

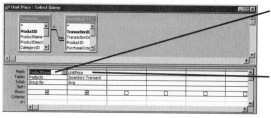

The first column tells Access to group products by product name.

The second column tells Access to calculate the average unit price.

You can summarize the results of a query by calculating any of the following statistical measures for a field in the query result's dynaset:

Summary operator	What it does
Avg	Calculates the average of a field's nonblank entries.
Count	Counts the number of nonblank field entries in the query result's dynaset.
Expression	Indicates an expression in the Field row by using at least one of the other summary operators.
First	Returns the first record's field entry.
Last	Returns the last record's field entry.
Max	Finds the largest value in a field's nonblank entries in the query result's dynaset.
Min	Finds the smallest value in a field's nonblank entries in the query result's dynaset.
StDev	Calculates the standard deviation of nonblank field entries.
Sum	Calculates the total of a field's entries.
Var	Calculates the variance of nonblank field entries.
Where	Allows criteria in the Criteria rows to narrow down the records to the query.

You must summarize or group each field

If you choose to summarize the records that make up a query result, you must choose either the Group By operator or one of the summary operators described in the preceding table for each field in the query design grid.

Reusing an Existing Query

To reuse a query—for example, when the database information changes—display the Database Window, click the Query toolbar button, and double-click the query. Access displays a Datasheet View window with the query results information. If your query is complex or your database is large, Access may take a while to complete the query.

Redesigning a Query

You can change the design of a query. Open the query (as just described), and click the Design toolbar button. Access displays the Query Design View window. You make the changes you want and then close the window, saving your changes.

continues

99

Query *(continued)*

Printing Query Results

To print query results, choose the File menu's Print command or click the Print toolbar button. Note that **reports** provide a more elaborate way to get printed copies of the information in a dynaset.

Query Design Grid

The grid you see at the bottom of the Query Design View window is called the query design grid. You enter information in it that Access needs to perform the query.

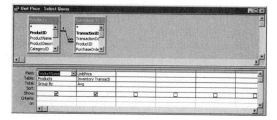

Query Query

A query query is a **query** of a query. In other words, it's a query in which you don't query a **table;** you query a query instead. All you have to do is select the query (rather than the table) as the **object** with data you want to query.

RDBMS

RDBMS stands for relational database management system. A relational database, such as Access, stores its data in **tables.** There are other types of databases; you create flat file databases in spreadsheet programs like Microsoft Excel and Lotus 1-2-3.

Record Locks

In a multiuser environment, Access locks a **record** when it's being edited by a user. By locking the record, Access prevents another user from simultaneously editing the record. The way this feature works is determined by the Multiuser/**ODBC** settings. You can change these settings by choosing the Tools menu's Options command, clicking the Advanced tab, and then using this tab's buttons and boxes. Because the use of record locks is somewhat complicated, however, it might be a good idea to take a look at the Access user documentation.

Records

A record is what gets stored in the rows of a **table**. It contains values for one or more **fields**.

Record Selectors

Access uses symbols or icons to convey useful information about the records in a **table**:

Symbol	What it means
🖉	Current record has been changed, but changes haven't been saved.
✳	Empty row for the next record.
▶	Current record that either hasn't been changed or whose changes have already been saved.

Referential Integrity

Referential integrity simply means that you can't enter a **record** in a related **table** unless the record ties, or connects, to a record in the **primary table**. Suppose that you've created a two-table database that tracks customers and the projects for a customer. In this situation, you might want to ensure that no project can be entered for a customer who isn't already described in the customer table. To ensure this referential integrity, close all objects and follow these steps:

1 Choose the Tools menu's Relationships command. Access displays the Relationships window.

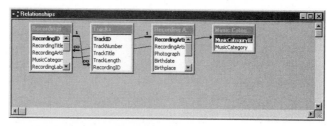

2 Double-click the relationship line that connects the tables' **common fields**. Access displays the Edit Relationships dialog box.

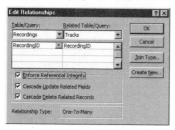

3 Select the Enforce Referential Integrity check box.

SEE ALSO Relationships

Relationships

You can tell Access how **tables** connect, or relate. For example, if you created a customer **database,** you might describe the relationship between customer table **records** and customer order table records. If you created a students database, you might describe the relationship between student table records and course grade table records.

Defining a Relationship

To describe the relationship between a **primary table** and any related tables, follow these steps:

1 Close all objects and choose the Tools menu's Relationships command. Access displays the Relationships window.

2 If the tables for which you want to define relationships don't show, choose Show Table from the Relationships menu. Access displays the Show Table dialog box.

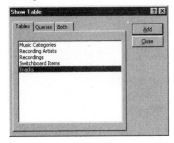

3 Select the tables for which you will define relationships by clicking them and then clicking Add.

4 Click Close. Access closes the Show Table dialog box and shows any existing relationships by drawing a line between two tables' common **fields.**

continues

Relationships *(continued)*

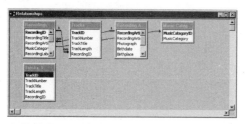

5 To define a relationship between two tables, drag the **common field** in the primary table to the common field in the related table. Access displays the Edit Relationships dialog box.

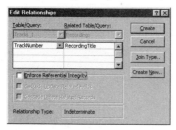

6 Select the Enforce Referential Integrity check box if you think that **referential integrity** is a good concept.

7 Click Create.

Deleting a Relationship

To delete a relationship between two tables, select the relationship line and then press Delete. You should be careful about deleting relationships, by the way. You may have other objects—queries, for example—that depend on the relationship.

Cascading referential integrity

The Cascade Update Related Fields and Cascade Delete Related Records check boxes relate to cascading referential integrity, which is a powerful and somewhat dangerous form of referential integrity. With cascading referential integrity, Access will delete and update records in related tables to maintain referential integrity.

Renaming Database Files

You use either Windows Explorer or My Computer to rename database **files**. To rename a file after you've started Windows Explorer, follow these steps:

1 Click the disk (or drive) with the file.

2 Click the folder and, if necessary, the subfolder that contains the file.

3 Right-click the file.

4 Choose the shortcut menu's Rename command.

5 Type a new name for the file.

6 Press Enter.

SEE ALSO   Filenames

Renaming Objects

To rename a database **object**, right-click the object in the **Database Window**. Then choose the shortcut menu's Rename command, type a new name for the object, and press Enter.

When you choose Rename, Access places the object name in an editable text box.

SEE ALSO   Saving Databases and Objects

Replacing Record Fields

To find a specific **record** and replace the contents of one of its **fields,** display a **form** that shows the record or display the **datasheet** for the **table** that stores the record. Then choose the Edit menu's Replace command.

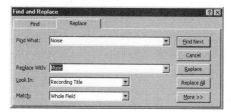

1 Enter the text you're looking for in the Find What text box.

2 Use the Look In box to specify which field to search. Although searching only the current field is faster, you have to ensure that the insertion point is in the field that contains the data.

3 Use the Match drop-down list box to tell Access whether what you're looking for starts the field, is somewhere within the field, or makes up the entire field.

4 Click More for other options: whether to search the table up, down, or both ways and whether to match the case and formatting of the text you've entered. Access normally ignores both case and formatting.

5 Click Find Next to start and restart the search.

6 Click Replace to replace the occurrence. Or click Replace All to replace all the occurrences.

Wildcards

You can use **wildcard characters** in your Find What entry. The ? character represents any single character. The * character represents any single character or any combination of characters. The # character represents any single digit.

SEE ALSO   Finding Records

Replica

A replica is just a copy of a single database **object** or a copy of a lot of database objects. You create replicas when you want to work with a database on more than one computer. For example; you might want to take a database you use on your desktop computer at the office and work with the database at home on your laptop computer. Access makes it easier to create replicas and then synchronize them with the original database. (By synchronizing, both the replica and original database are made up-to-date.) To create a replica, choose from the Tools menu's Replication submenu commands.

Reports

Reports summarize the information in **tables** or **queries**. A report is one of the three available methods for viewing table data and query results. (The other two methods are **forms** and **datasheets**.) Like a datasheet, a report shows multiple **records**. The difference is that you can choose the format a report uses to summarize and show your table data. A datasheet, in comparison, shows table data in a table.

Creating a Column Report

To create a report that lists only table records, follow these steps:

1 Open the **database** to which the report should be added. Access displays the **Database Window**.

2 Click Reports.

3 Click New.

4 Select the Report Wizard entry from the list box.

5 Open the drop-down list box, and select the table or query for which you want to create a report.

6 Click OK.

continues

Reports *(continued)*

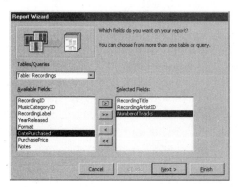

7 Select the fields you want. You can select individual fields by clicking the field in the Available Fields list box and then clicking the > button. You can select all the fields by clicking the >> button. You can remove a field from the Selected Fields list box by clicking it and then clicking the < button. You can remove all the fields from the Selected Fields list box by clicking the << button. If you want, select another table or query from the Tables/Queries drop-down list box to add more fields to the report.

8 Click Next. Access asks how you want to group your records.

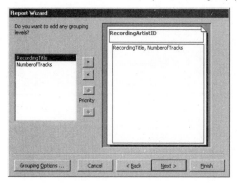

9 By clicking fields and pressing the >, <, ↑, and ↓ buttons, determine the main and subgroupings for your report.

10 Click Next. Access asks how you want to sort records within each grouping.

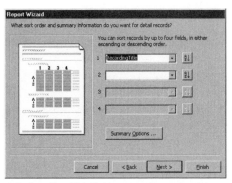

11 Specify which fields to use for sorting the records by using the drop-down list boxes.

12 Click Next. Access asks how you want your report laid out.

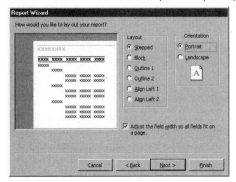

13 Select the options that correspond to the layout and orientation you want.

14 Click Next. Tell Access which style of report you want. Preview the different style options by clicking them.

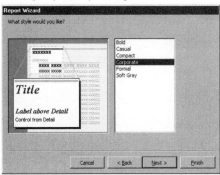

continues

Reports *(continued)*

15 Click Next. Access asks what name it should use for the report object. You can also choose whether to preview the report, modify its design, or get help in working with the report.

16 Click Finish.

Previewing a Report

You can produce a report and preview it on your screen by opening the database so that the Database Window is shown, clicking Reports, and then double-clicking the report. When you do, Access displays a window that shows the printed pages of the report.

Use the Zoom toolbar button to magnify and then reduce the size of the page displayed in the Print Preview window.

If your report doesn't fit on the screen or on a single page, you can page through it by using the page selector buttons or the page number box, which appear in the bottom left corner of the window.

Printing a Report

To print a report, follow these steps:

1 Preview the report in the Print Preview window.

2 Choose the File menu's Print command. Access displays the Print dialog box. Or click the Print toolbar button, and Access just starts printing.

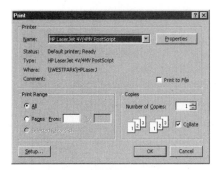

3 Use the Print Range options to print a portion of the report (for example, pages 2-8).

4 Enter a number in the Number Of Copies box to print multiple copies of the report.

Closing a Report

Close the report by clicking its Close button. Or choose the File menu's Close command.

Using an Existing Report

To use a report you've already created, preview it as described earlier.

Redesigning a Report

You can change the design of a report manually. Open the Database Window, click Reports, and click Design View. Access displays the Report Design View window and the Report Design toolbox. You use these elements to modify the selected report.

Although redesigning a report isn't terribly difficult, it can be time-consuming. If you want to redesign a report, try creating a new report with the Report Wizard instead.

SEE ALSO **Mailing Labels**

Saving Data Access Pages

You can save data access pages in roughly the same manner as you save other Access objects. The only real difference is that you save data access pages to an HTML file on your hard drive or web server instead of into your Access database. To save a data access page, follow these steps:

1 Select or open your data access page, and then choose the File menu's Save As command.

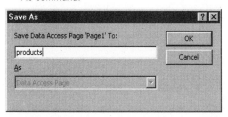

2 In the Save As dialog box, specify the name of the new file, and click OK.

3 In the Save As Data Access Page dialog box, specify where you want to place your page by using either the shortcut icons (**History, My Documents, Desktop, Favorites,** or **Web Folders**) or the Save In box.

4 Give the new web page a filename in the File Name box.

5 Verify that the Save As Type box indicates that you're saving a data access page.

6 Click OK.

SEE ALSO Saving Databases and Objects

Saving Databases and Objects

If you've worked with other applications, you'll see that saving database **objects** to disk works a little differently from what you might expect.

Saving Changes to Records

If you add a **record** to a **table** or change the contents of some **field,** you'll want the addition or change saved. Because Access knows this, it saves your additions or changes automatically when you move to another record or when you tell it that you want to add a new record. In other words, you don't save changes to records; Access does (which means that you may inadvertently do things that cause Access to save record changes you don't want to make).

Saving Changes to an Object

You can save objects you create and save changes to the design of existing objects. Choose the File menu's Save command, or click the Save toolbar button. If this is the first time you've saved an object, Access will ask you to enter an object name. Object names can be as long as 64 characters, including spaces.

If you make changes to an existing object's design and want to keep both the old and new versions, choose the File menu's Save As command and enter a new name for the new object.

SEE ALSO   Back Up; Renaming Objects

Select Query

A select query is a **query** that selects and sometimes summarizes **records.** The queries I describe in the **Query** entry, for example, are all select queries. Access uses other types of queries, however: **action queries,** for example, and crosstab queries.

SEE ALSO   Crosstab

Self-Join

A self-join is another type of table combination, or join. It occurs when a table connects to itself. Refer to the Access user documentation for more information.

SEE ALSO   Joining Tables

Shortcut Menus

Access is smart enough to know which commands make sense in which situations. It also knows which commands you, as a user, are most likely to use in these situations, and will display them on a shortcut menu. To see a shortcut menu, right-click the mouse. (Remember that you use the left mouse button for selecting menus, commands, dialog box elements, and assorted and sundry items.)

Shortcut menus are fast and convenient. They're more complicated to write about and read than they are to use. By far the best way to learn to use them is to experiment by right-clicking various objects. You can always cancel a shortcut menu by clicking something else on the screen.

Spelling

To check the spelling of words in **fields,** select the field and then choose the Tools menu's Spelling command or click the Spelling toolbar button. If Access finds no misspelled words, it displays a message box simply telling you that it has checked the words in your selection. If Access does find a misspelled word, it displays the Spelling dialog box, which you use to control the way Access spell-checks and what it does when it finds a possible error.

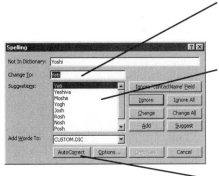

Although Access suggests an alternative spelling in the Change To text box, you can edit whatever Access suggests.

Other words that are spelled similarly to what you entered may appear in the Suggestions list box. You can select any of these words by clicking them.

You can add words you misspell often and their corrected versions to the AutoCorrect list of common mistakes.

Spelling Dialog Box Buttons

After Access finds a potentially misspelled word, you use the buttons in the Spelling dialog box to indicate what Access should do:

Button	What it does
Ignore	Ignores only this occurrence of the word.
Ignore Field	Ignores this field.
Ignore All	Ignores this and every other occurrence of the word.
Change	Changes this occurrence of the word to what the Change To text box shows.
Change All	Changes this and every other occurrence of the word to what the Change To text box shows.
Add	Adds the word to the spelling dictionary named in the Add Words To drop-down list box.
Suggest	Looks for similarly spelled words in the Access spelling dictionary and the custom dictionary named in the Add Words To drop-down list box.

continues

Spelling *(continued)*

If Access can't find your word

You can use the **wildcard characters** ? and * in the Change To box to find words spelled similarly to what you enter. You can use the * character to represent any combination of characters, and you can use the ? character to represent any single character. For example, if you're trying to spell a word that starts with the letters *Colo* but you—and Access—don't know which letters follow, type *Colo** in the Change To text box; then click Suggest. Access will find all the words in its dictionary that start with the letters *Colo*.

SQL

SQL (pronounced "sequel") stands for Structured Query Language. It's a database sublanguage (similar to a programming language) that databases understand and that you use (or that the database uses) to retrieve data from the database.

When you create a **query**, Access creates the SQL statements that describe your query. If you're interested in this concept, you can see what the SQL statements look like by choosing the View menu's SQL View command when you've displayed the Query Object window.

Access now allows you to convert your database to a Microsoft SQL Server database. Choose the Tools menu's Database Utilities command and the submenu's Upsizing Wizard command.

Connecting to a SQL database?

If you're planning to use Access to connect to a SQL database, you will need to have installed the appropriate **ODBC** driver when you installed Access.

Starting Access

You start a Windows-based **program** such as Access either manually or as part of starting Windows.

Starting Access Manually

To start Access manually, click the Start button, choose Programs, and then choose Microsoft Access. (You may find it in the Microsoft Office folder.)

Starting Access Automatically

If you want to start Access every time you start Windows, just follow these steps:

1 Click the Start button, choose Settings, and then choose Taskbar.

2 In the Taskbar Properties dialog box, click the Start Menu Programs tab.

3 Click Add, and then click Browse.

4 Find the Access application icon (it's normally in the Program Files/Microsoft Office folder). Double-click it.

5 Click Next to close the dialog box, and then click the StartUp folder. Click Next again.

6 Type *Access* to make its name appear on the StartUp menu, and then click Finish.

After You've Started Access

After you—or Windows—have started Access, Access asks whether you want to create a new database by using either a blank database or the **Database Wizard** or whether you want to open an existing database. Access lists databases you've recently opened. To open one of the listed databases, double-click it.

Subform

A subform is a **form** attached to another form. You typically create a subform when you want to show related records from two objects. The form to which this new subform is attached is called a main form.

If you base the main form and the subform on **tables,** the main form will probably show a **primary table** and the subform will show the related table. The **relationship** between the main form table and the subform table will be one-to-many.

continues

Subform *(continued)*

Creating a Form that Uses a Subform

To attach a subform to a main form, follow these steps:

1 Open the **Database Window.**

2 Click Forms.

3 Click New.

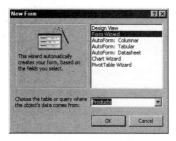

4 Select the Form Wizard entry from the list box.

5 Open the drop-down list box, and select the object on which the main form should be based.

6 Click OK.

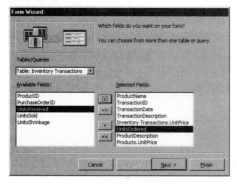

7 Select the **fields** you want in the order they should appear on the main form. You can select individual fields by clicking the field in the Available Fields list box and then clicking the > button. You can select all the available fields by clicking the >> button. You can remove a field from the Selected Fields list box by clicking it and choosing the < button. You can remove all the fields from the Selected Fields list box by clicking the << button.

8 Indicate which table or **query** the subform should be based on by selecting the object from the Tables/Queries drop-down list box.

9 Select the fields you want in the order they should appear on the subform. This process works the same way as selecting fields for the main form (as described in step 7). For example, you can select individual fields by clicking the field in the Available Fields list box and then clicking the > button.

10 Click Next. Access asks how you want to view your form.

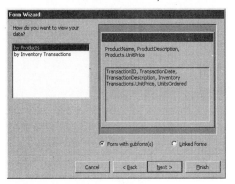

11 Select the object whose fields should appear on the main form. (This will be the primary table.)

12 Verify that the Form With Subform(s) option is selected. If it isn't, select it.

13 Click Next. Access asks how you want your form laid out.

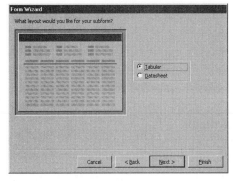

14 Select an option, and click Next. Access asks how you want your form to look.

continues

Subform (continued)

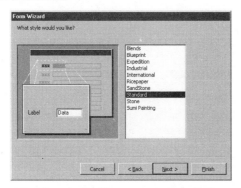

15 Select the "look" you want from the list box.

16 Click Next. Access asks what name Access should use for the main form and subform and whether you want to start using the form or want instead to redesign some of the form by fiddling with its **control objects**.

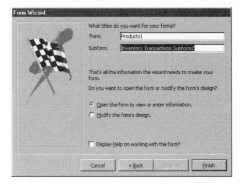

17 Replace the suggested name if you want, but you probably don't need to redesign the form.

18 Click Finish. Access displays your new form.

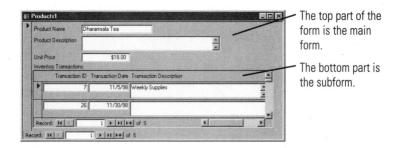

The top part of the form is the main form.

The bottom part is the subform.

Switchboard

When you use the **Database Wizard** to create a database, Access creates a set of menus you can use to work with the objects.

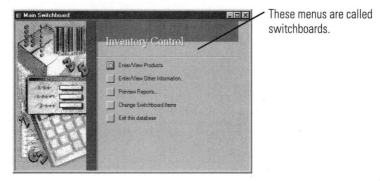

These menus are called switchboards.

Switching Tasks

To multitask (run multiple applications) in Windows, use the Taskbar. Just click the name of the application you want.

Easy switching

You can cycle through the programs you're running by using the keyboard. Press Alt+Tab to return to the last active program. Or hold down the Alt key and repeatedly press Tab to see a message box that lists the running programs, and then release the Alt and Tab keys when the message box names the programs you want to switch to.

Tables

A table is the container a relational database such as Access uses for holding data. Each table stores **records** with the same **fields.**

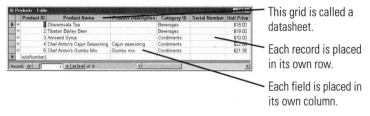

This grid is called a datasheet.

Each record is placed in its own row.

Each field is placed in its own column.

Creating a Table with the Table Wizard

To create a table with the Table Wizard, follow these steps:

1 Open the database to which the table should be added. Or create the database if it doesn't yet exist. Open the **Database Window.**

2 Click Tables.

3 Click New.

4 Select the Table Wizard entry from the list box, and then click OK.

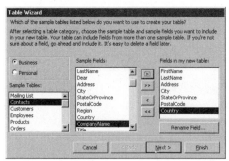

5 Click the Business or Personal option button to tell Access which list of sample tables it should display.

6 Select an entry from the Sample Tables list box. If you were building a customer contacts table, for example, you would select the Contacts entry.

7 Select the fields you want. You can select individual table fields by clicking the field in the Sample Fields list box and then clicking the > button. You can select all the table's fields by clicking the >> button. You can remove a field from the Fields In My New Table list box by clicking it and then clicking the < button. You can remove all the fields from the Fields In My New Table list box by clicking the << button.

8 Click Next. Access asks you to name the table and specify whether Access should specify the **primary key.**

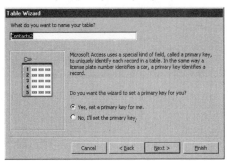

9 Name the table.

10 Click the option that indicates whether Access should set the primary key for you. (If you don't have an appropriate primary key field in your table, Access will add an **AutoNumber** field and use it as the primary key.)

11 Click Next. Access asks you whether your new table is related to any of the existing tables in your database. The dialog box lists any obvious relationships Access has already identified.

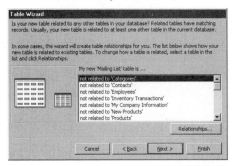

12 If a relationship exists but Access hasn't identified it, select the related table and click Relationships. Access displays the Relationships dialog box.

continues

Tables *(continued)*

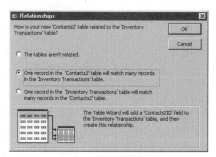

13 Describe the relationship by clicking the appropriate option and then clicking OK. (If the new table you're creating is the "one," or primary, table in a one-to-many relationship, click the second option. If the new table you're creating is the "many," or related, table in a one-to-many relationship, click the third option.)

14 If necessary, repeat steps 12 and 13 to describe any other relationships. Then click Next. Access asks whether you want to modify the table design, add records by using a datasheet, or add records by using a **form** that Access will create for you.

15 Indicate whether you want to modify the table design or add records, and then click Finish.

Creating a Table from Scratch

To create a table, follow these steps:

1 Open the database to which the table should be added, or create the database if it doesn't yet exist. Open the Database Window.

2 Click Tables.

3 Click New.

4 Select Design View, and then click OK. Access displays the table's Design view in a window.

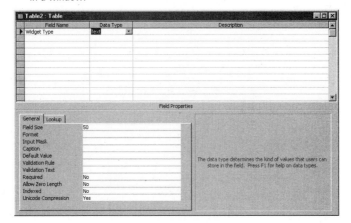

5 Enter in the Field Name column a name for each of the table's fields.

6 Open the Data Type drop-down list, and select a **data type.**

7 Describe the field by using the Description text box. (Access displays this description on the status bar whenever the field is selected in a datasheet or form.)

8 Repeat steps 5 through 7 for each of the table's fields.

9 Select a primary key field, and then choose the Edit menu's Primary Key command.

10 Close the Table Design View window—for example, by clicking its Close button.

11 When Access asks, give the table an **object name.**

continues

125

Tables *(continued)*

Filling a Table with a Datasheet View Window

To fill the table with data, you can use a datasheet. Choose the View menu's Datasheet command. If Access asks about saving the changes to your table, click OK.

Note that you can also use a form to fill a table with data.

Copying data

You can copy the preceding record's field contents into the same field in the current record by pressing Ctrl+' (the Ctrl key and the apostrophe key).

Editing Data in a Table's Datasheet

To edit the data in a table's datasheet, simply double-click the field to select its contents. Erase the selected field's contents by pressing Delete. Or replace the selected field's contents by typing. To insert something, reposition the insertion point by pressing the Left and Right arrow keys or click the mouse and then type. Access inserts whatever you type at the insertion point. Press the Backspace key to erase the character preceding the insertion point.

Opening an Existing Table

To view an existing table's information in a datasheet window, open the Database Window, click Tables, and then double-click the table. Access displays a datasheet window with the table information.

Redesigning a Table

You can change the design of a table by adding and removing columns, or fields. Select the table, and click Design. Access displays the design view of the table. It uses rows to describe each field in the table.

To delete a column, or a field, from a table, select the row that describes the column and then choose the Edit menu's Delete Row command or press Delete.

To insert a field in the table, select the field in front of which the field should be inserted. Then choose the Insert menu's Rows command, and fill in the blank row that Access inserts.

Changing field properties

You can change field properties, but you have to be careful. If you reduce a field's field size from 50 characters to 10, for example, any original field entries longer than 10 characters will get cut off. If you change a field's data type, you may lose data if part of the original field entry won't fit in the new data type. You also have to be careful when you start fooling around with elements such as primary keys and indexes. If you create a "No duplicates" index and the table has duplicate field entries, Access will remove the duplicate entries. I should mention that Access won't make a table design change that leads to data loss without asking you whether you're aware of the possible data loss.

Printing a Table

To **print** a table's information, first open it. Then choose the File menu's Print command or click the Print toolbar button. Note that Access **reports** provide a more elaborate way to produce printed copies of the information in a table.

Closing a Table

When you finish entering or editing table data, close the table by clicking the Close button or choosing the File menu's Close command. Access returns you to the Database Window.

SEE ALSO   Field Property; Importing Data

Table Wizard

The Table Wizard creates **tables** almost automatically. All you do is answer a handful of simple questions presented in some dialog boxes. For more information, refer to the preceding entry.

Toolbox

If you view a **report** or **form** object in **Design view,** you'll see the toolbox. It provides a series of buttons you can click to add **control objects** to forms and reports. The following table lists the tools and what they do. If you have questions, your best bet is probably to use a **Control Wizard,** which will step you through the process of adding or modifying control objects.

continues

Toolbox *(continued)*

Button	What it does
	Selects a control object so that you can move and resize it.
	Turns on and off the Control Wizards.
	Adds a label.
	Adds a text box.
	Groups a set of options control objects—for example, option buttons.
	Adds a toggling button you can select and deselect. If selected, the button appears pushed in.
	Adds an option button.
	Adds a check box.
	Adds a combo box.
	Adds a list box.
	Adds a command button such as you might use for a **macro button.**
	Adds a picture, a **graph,** or an OLE object that isn't stored in a **table.**
	Adds an unbound object frame.
	Adds a picture, a graph, or an OLE object that is stored in a table.
	Adds a page break.
	Adds tabs to the form.
	Adds a **subform** to a **form** or **report** or embeds a report in another existing report.
	Adds a line.
	Adds a rectangle.
	Displays a list box of any custom controls you can add to the form or report.

Undo

You can undo your editing changes to a **record** or a **field,** and you can often undo your design changes to a database object. To reverse the changes you've just made, click the Undo toolbar button.

Unicode

This encoding standard lets computers work with practically any characters used on a computer. Unicode therefore works with most of the languages in the world and with just about any mathematical or technical symbols you will see. Microsoft Office 2000 programs, including Access, support the Unicode standard.

URL

The URL, or uniform resource locator, specifies how you find an Internet resource such as a **World Wide Web** page. A URL has four parts: the service, or protocol; the server name; the path; and the document, or file, name.

A Sample URL Explained

Let me explain what each of these things is, by using a real-life web page—the one that provides information about the Executive Office of the President.

http://www.whitehouse.gov/WH/EOP/html/principals.html

http:// identifies this resource as part of the World Wide Web.

www.whitehouse.gov/ identifies the server.

WH/EOP/html/ names the folder and subfolders of the World Wide Web document.

principals.html names the World Wide Web document.

V

Validation Rules

A validation rule is an **expression** Access uses to evaluate an entry that you or someone else attempts to place in a **field**. If what gets entered into the field matches the expression, Access allows the entry. If what gets entered into the field doesn't match the expression, Access doesn't allow the entry.

One other thing: Access validates only field entries. If nothing gets entered into a field, Access doesn't do any validation.

Validation Comparison Operators

Validation rules use **logical operators**. The following table describes the logical operators available for use in validation rules:

Operator	Valid field entries must be
=	Equal to. For example, the validation rule *=100* means that the field entry must equal 100. The expression *="CA"* means that the field entry must be the two characters CA.
>=	Greater than or equal to. For example, the validation rule *>=100* means that the field entry must be greater than or equal to 100.
>	Greater than. For example, the validation rule *>100* means that the field entry must be greater than 100.
<=	Less than or equal to. For example, the validation rule *<=100* means that the field entry must be less than or equal to 100.
<	Less than. For example, the validation rule *<100* means that the field entry must be less than 100.
<>	Not equal to. For example, the validation rule *<>100* means that the field entry must not equal 100.
And	Meet two validation rules. For example, the validation rule *>=100 AND <1000* means that the field entry must be greater than or equal to 100 and less than 1000.
Or	Meet one of the validation rules described. For example, the validation rule *="CO" OR ="WA"* means that the field entry must either be the two characters CO or the two characters WA.
Like	Composed of specified characters. For example, the validation rule *Like "??"* means that the field entry can use only two characters. The validation rule *Like "###"* means that the field entry can use only three numbers.

Validation rules ignore case

Validation rules ignore case (uppercase vs. lowercase). The validation rule ="CA" allows the field entries CA, ca, cA, and Ca, for example.

> **SEE ALSO   Field Property**

Views

You can look at database **objects** from more than a single perspective: you can look at **tables** and **reports,** for example, from either a Design view or a Datasheet view. You can look at **forms** from a Design view, a Datasheet view, or a Form view. You can also look at **queries** from a Design view, from a SQL view, or from a Datasheet view.

Datasheet and Form Views

One way of looking at a database object is by looking at the actual data the object stores or retrieves. If the data from a table or query appears in a **datasheet,** for example, this view is called the Datasheet view of the table or query.

If the data for a form appears in a form, this view is called the Form view of the form. Although this concept might seem confusing, you can also view the data for a form in a datasheet—the Datasheet view of the form.

Design View

Another way of looking at an object is by looking at the description of the object. This is called the Design view. When you're creating a table by describing its **fields,** for example, you'll be looking not at the table's data but at the table's design.

SQL View

The SQL view of a query object shows the SQL statements that describe a query.

continues

Views *(continued)*

Switching Between Views

Access has a View button on the toolbar that changes function—Design view, Datasheet view, Form view, and even SQL view—according to circumstances.

You can look at a database object's Design view in a window by clicking the Design View toolbar button.

You can look at a database object's data view in a **datasheet** window by clicking the Datasheet View toolbar button.

You can look at a database object's Data view in a form window if a form has been designed by clicking the Form View toolbar button.

The down arrow at the right end of the View button opens a drop-down list box of all the possible views of the object displayed in the active document window.

Visual Basic

Visual Basic is the programming language that is built into Access. For information about Visual Basic, see your Access user documentation.

SEE ALSO   **Macro Buttons; Macros; Modules**

Web Folder

The Web Folder shortcut icon, which appears in the New Data Access Page dialog box, lists web server locations you can use for storing and retrieving **data access pages.**

SEE ALSO   **Saving Data Access Pages**

Wildcard Characters

These characters can stand for other characters in an **expression.** The most common wildcard characters are the question mark (?) and the asterisk (*) symbols. A question mark can stand for any single character. An asterisk can stand for any single character or any group of characters. Access also supplies a number (#) wildcard character that can stand for any single digit.

You can indicate that you're looking for specific characters by in-cluding the characters in brackets—[and]. For example, the entry *N[ie]lson* would find both *Nelson* and *Nilson*.

You can specify that you don't want to find the letters inside the brackets by preceding the characters with an exclamation point. For example, the entry N[!e]lson would find *Nilson, Nolson*—any six-letter entry that started with an *N* and ended with *lson* except *Nelson*.

You can also specify that you want to find a range of letters inside the brackets by using the hyphen. For example, the entry *N[a-i]lson* would find entries such as *Nalson, Nelson* and *Nilson* but not *Nolson*.

If you're interested in the wildcard concept, take a peek at the **Validation Rules** entry and at the **Query** entry. They both show more examples of wildcard usage.

Wizards

Access supplies wizards that help you create both your database and database **objects**. Because this Pocket Guide is a quick-help book, I'll almost always describe how to accomplish a task by using an Access wizard.

SEE ALSO   Database Wizard; Forms; Reports; Tables

World Wide Web

The World Wide Web (also known as WWW or simply the Web) is a set of multimedia documents that are connected so that you can jump from one document to another by using **hyperlinks,** usually with just a click. The multimedia part means that you're not limited to words: you can place pictures, sounds, and even video clips in a web document.

To view a World Wide Web document, you must have a web browser. Popular Web browsers include Microsoft Internet Explorer and Netscape Navigator.

continues

World Wide Web *(continued)*

If you want to start exploring the Web, try using a search engine like Yahoo! It provides a folder of thousands of different World Wide Web sites. You can find Yahoo! at the URL address *http://www.yahoo.com*.

Access makes it easy for you to insert hyperlinks to Access databases and objects in web documents.

SEE ALSO   Data Access Page

Troubleshooting

Got a problem? Starting on the next page are solutions to the problems that sometimes plague new users of Microsoft Access. You'll be on your way—and safely out of trouble—in no time.

Data Entry

You Get a Duplicate Key Error

If you get a duplicate key error, it means that you've entered a value in a **primary key** field for the **record** that some other record already uses. Because the primary key value can't be duplicated, this contradiction, in effect, triggers the error.

Use a different primary key value

Because duplicate primary key values can't exist, you simply need to use a different primary key value for the new record you're trying to add.

You Can't Enter a Calculated Field for a Table

The problem in this situation is that **tables** store only raw data. You don't use tables to calculate numbers or to store the results of calculations. Maybe you do want a calculation made, though. For example, a table that stores the quantities and unit prices of products ordered by a customer should logically calculate the order amount by multiplying the quantity by the unit price, but it doesn't. To know the order amount, you'll have to make the calculation yourself.

Create a query that uses the calculated field

You can create a **query** that makes the calculation you want in a **calculated field.** Note that you can use a query object to provide data to **forms,** to **reports,** and even to other queries. For all practical purposes, you can think of a query as a table.

You Can't Change a Locked Record

If you are using Microsoft Access in a multiuser environment, you may encounter **record locks:** if record locking is turned on, you can't change a record that some other user is editing. After all, if both you and the person in the next cubicle make changes to a **record,** Access doesn't know how to reconcile the changes when you both try to save them.

Wait awhile and try again

Access will unlock the record when whoever is editing it finishes. When the record is unlocked, you'll be able to see it and make whatever changes you want.

Editing etiquette

Because you lock records when you edit them, thereby preventing others from accessing them, minimize the time you spend editing a record. You don't want to display some record in a **form,** for example, ponder possible changes for 20 minutes, and then head off for a 2-hour lunch with the form still showing the record on your screen.

You Can't Sort Table Records

Access doesn't sort table **records** as you enter them.

Use the Quick Sort commands

To sort a table's records in ascending order based on some **field,** select the field and then click the Sort Ascending toolbar button.

To sort a table's records in descending order based on some field, select the field and then click the Sort Descending toolbar button.

Create a query

To sort a table's records in a more complicated order—such as based on several key fields—simply create a **select query.**

You can use a query **object** in all the same ways you use a table object. You can create **reports** that use query objects, for example, and you can create **forms** that you can use to fill a query object's **dynaset** (and, therefore, the queried tables) with data.

Query

You Want to Search for Text that Uses an Operator

If you want to search for a text string that includes an operator such as And or Or, you can't just enter the text string into the selection criteria row.

Enclose the text string in quotation marks

To search for a text string which uses a word that Access also uses as an operator, enclose the text string in quotation marks.

To search for the phrase *Rock and roll,* for example, you need to enter this string in quotation marks, as shown here.

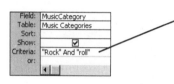

If you don't enclose the text string in quotation marks, Access assumes that the word which looks like an operator is an operator. In this case, for example, Access encloses the words *Rock* and *roll* in quotation marks because it assumes that you're looking for records with Project Description fields equal to "Rock" and "roll." Because no single field can contain two separate entries, this selection criteria never selects a record.

SEE ALSO   Query

Your Or Works Like an And

When you use more than a single criterion to select records in a **query,** it's easy to have criteria that you intend to have applied individually be applied collectively instead. The key concept to remember is that each row of selection criteria information in a **query design grid** describes a set of selection criteria that must all be met in order for records to be selected.

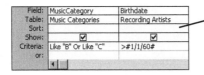

For a record to be selected in this query, the last name must start with the letter *B* or *C* and the birth date must fall after January 1, 1960. A record for someone with the last name Nelson and a birthday in 1959 won't get selected, for example, but neither will a record for someone with the last name Baker and a birthday in 1959.

For a record to be selected in this query, either the last name must start with the letter *B* or *C* or the birth date must fall after January 1, 1960. A record for someone with the last name Nelson and a birthday in 1969 will get selected, for example, because of the birth date. A record for someone with the last name Baker and a birthday in 1959 will get selected because of the last name.

Printing

You Want to Cancel a Printing Database

If you've told Access to **print** a database object that you realize you don't want to print, you may want to cancel the printing, particularly if the database object requires many pages on which to print.

Delete the print job

When Access prints a database object, it creates a print spool file it sends to Windows. Windows then prints this print spool file as well as any other spool files that Access and other applications have sent. To cancel a printing Access database object, therefore, follow these steps:

1 Click the Start button. Choose Settings and then Printers to display the Printers window.

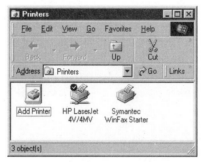

2 To display the print queue for the printer, double-click the printer icon for the printer you're using.

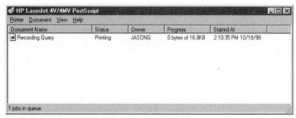

3 Click the printing Access database object.

4 Press Delete, or choose the Document menu's Cancel Printing command.

SEE ALSO Switching Tasks

Files

You Can't Save a Database

Access needs a certain amount of system resources, or memory, to save a database **file.** If your system resources get too low, therefore, you can run into a serious problem: you may not be able to save your database. Fortunately, as long as you keep your cool, this situation doesn't have to be a disaster. You have to free up system resources and then try resaving the database.

Close your other open programs

Switch to any of your other open **programs** and close them. Click their buttons on the Taskbar; or, if your Taskbar is not on top or visible, press Alt+Tab to switch to other programs' windows, and then choose the File menu's Exit command.

When you've closed all the other programs (and saved their documents, if that's appropriate), return to Access and try resaving the database you couldn't save earlier.

SEE ALSO **Saving Databases and Objects; Switching Tasks**

You Can't Find a File

Large hard disks make it easy to misplace a **file.** Fortunately, Windows provides an extremely powerful tool for finding lost files: the Find File program. Because Access **databases** are files, you can use Find File to locate lost databases.

Because Find File is so powerful and tremendously useful, I'm going to describe it in detail on the next page.

continues

You Can't Find a File *(continued)*

Use Find File

To start Find File, click the Start button, choose Find, and then choose Files Or Folders. Windows displays the Find: All Files dialog box.

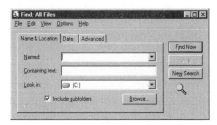

1 If you know the filename, enter it in the Named box. You can use wildcard characters as part of the filename.

2 Tell Windows where to look by using the Look In box.

3 Select the Include Subfolders check box if you want to look in both folders and subfolders.

4 To describe the last modification date of the file, click the Date tab.

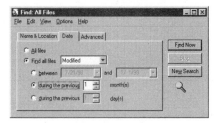

5 Or use the Advanced tab's options to describe some string of text in the file or the file size.

6 Click Find Now to start the search. Windows displays the Find: All Files window with a list of the files.

Multitasking

If you describe a sophisticated search—one that looks for a portion of text within files, for example—the search can take a long time (perhaps hours or even days). This situation doesn't have to be a problem, however. You can run other **programs** at the same time. All you need to do is start the other programs.

SEE ALSO Switching Tasks

You Accidentally Erase a File

If you erase or delete a file and later realize that you shouldn't have, not all is lost. The Recycle Bin stores deleted files. (Note that when the Recycle Bin eventually does fill up, Windows makes room for new deleted files in the Recycle Bin by removing the oldest deleted files, so you may not be able to restore very old files by using the Recycle Bin.)

Restore the file

To restore a file you've deleted, follow these steps:

1 Double-click the Recycle Bin icon to display the Recycle Bin window.

2 Select the file you want to restore.

3 Choose the File menu's Restore command.

SEE ALSO Database; Saving Databases and Objects

You Can't Remember Your Password

If you or someone else assigned a password to open a database file, you'll need to supply that password before you open the file. If you forget your password or can't seem to enter it correctly, Access won't let you open the database.

continues

You Can't Remember Your Password *(continued)*

 Try a password with different-case letters

Access differentiates passwords on the basis of the letter-case. The following words, for example, are all different passwords from the Access point of view: Wathers, wATHERS, and WATHERS. For this reason, if you think that you know the password, try changing the lowercase letters to uppercase letters and vice versa. You may have entered the password with a different combination of uppercase and lowercase letters than you think. (This situation can occur, for instance, if you accidentally press the Caps Lock key before entering the password.)

 Get help from the database administrator

If you've tried the preceding technique and still can't enter your password, you need help from the database administrator. This person will probably be the same person who originally provided your password and user name.

SEE ALSO Opening Databases; Saving Databases and Objects

Your Hard Disk Is Full

If your hard disk begins to fill up, you should either free up some space or buy a bigger disk—for two reasons. First, Windows likes a certain amount of free disk space to run "virtual memory." Second, some Windows-based **programs** return an "application error" if they encounter a full hard disk.

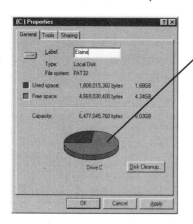

To check your free disk space, start Windows Explorer, click the hard disk's icon, and then choose the File menu's Properties command. The General tab in the Properties dialog box includes a pie chart that shows the amount of free disk space.

Empty the Recycle Bin and reduce its capacity

The Recycle Bin, as you may know, stores deleted files. Windows allocates a specific percentage of your disk space—the default percentage is 10 percent—to store the Recycle Bin's files.

One way to recover some disk space is to empty the Recycle Bin or at least delete some of its files. Then, after taking either of these actions, you can reduce the Recycle Bin's capacity. To do this, follow these steps:

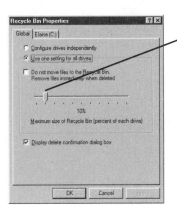

1 Display the Recycle Bin window (by either double-clicking the Recycle Bin icon or opening the Recycle Bin by using Windows Explorer).

2 Choose the File menu's Empty Recycle Bin command.

3 Close the Recycle Bin.

4 Right-click the Recycle Bin icon.

5 Choose the shortcut menu's Properties command.

6 Move the slide control to the left so that the Recycle Bin reserves less space.

continues

145

Your Hard Disk Is Full *(continued)*

 ### Erase any unneeded files

Another way to free up disk space is to remove individual **files** from the disk by using the File menu's Delete command in Windows Explorer. Then remove the files from the Recycle Bin— I told you how to do that in the preceding section. (If you want to save the files, you can first copy them to a floppy disk or other storage place.)

It's not generally a good idea to remove files you didn't create. For example, you and Windows or you and some program might have different ideas about whether a file is needed.

You Can't Save a File to a Floppy Disk

If you attempt to save a database file or copy a database file to a floppy disk but can't, you can try several things.

 ### Unprotect the floppy disk

If you get a message which says that a disk is write-protected, you won't be able to save, or write, a database file to the disk until you unprotect the disk.

To write to a 3.5-inch floppy disk, verify that the disk doesn't have a square hole in its top-right corner when you're holding the disk so that you can read its label. If a square hole *is* there, turn the floppy disk over and move the slide that covers the hole.

To write to a 5.25-inch floppy disk, verify that the floppy disk has a notch. If a piece of tape or an adhesive tab is covering this notch, remove it.

Why the write-protection?

Before you write to a previously write-protected floppy disk, you may want to consider the reasons someone protected the disk. The disk may have on it some information that shouldn't be written over.

Format the floppy if needed

If you get a message that Windows or a Windows-based application, such as Access, can't read a disk, the reason may be that the disk isn't formatted. If you know that it's not formatted or you don't need any information that's on the floppy disk, you can format the floppy disk. (For practical purposes, formatting it destroys everything that's on it.) Refer to the Windows user documentation for information about how to do this task.

Verify there's room

A floppy disk doesn't have much space for storing information, compared to a hard disk. Your database file will soon quite likely grow too large to fit on a single floppy disk. In this event, you'll need to **back up** the database file to a multiple number of floppy disks; to a mass storage device, like a Jaz, SparQ, or Zip drive; or to a tape.

You Can't Get Access to Respond

A bug in Access or some other program can (but is unlikely to) cause the application to stop responding. If it happens, you won't be able to choose menu commands, and you may not be able to move the mouse pointer.

 ### Terminate the unresponsive program

Unfortunately, if a **program** is truly unresponsive—if it ignores your keyboard and mouse actions—you can't do anything to make it start responding again. When that's the case, however, you can press Ctrl+Alt+Del.

Ctrl+Alt+Del (you press the three keys simultaneously) tells Windows to check the active program for responsiveness. Windows makes this check and tells you whether the program is, in fact, "not responding."

To terminate the program, select it and click End Task. To remove the Close Program dialog box from the screen, click Close.

You should consider the possibility that Access is simply busy instead. Access, for example, may be running a **macro** or a **module.** Another program may be printing to a spool file or executing another command you've given it. (If the hard disk light is flickering, something is happening!)

You Can't Get Access to Respond *(continued)*

Terminating programs with Windows NT

The preceding description explains how to terminate an unresponsive program, or application, with Windows 95 or Windows 98. In Windows NT and Windows 2000, the steps work slightly differently. Press Ctrl+Alt+Del. Click the Task Manager button. Select the unresponsive program. Then click End Task.

You Get an Application Error

Sometimes a program, or application, asks Windows to do the impossible. When that happens—which isn't often, thankfully—Windows displays a message box which says that an application error, or program error, has occurred.

Close the program

When Windows alerts you to a program error, you usually have two choices: Close and Details. You should choose Close.

Windows may also (rarely) give you the option of ignoring the error. Even in this case, the most prudent choice is still to close the **program.**

By the way, if you have been working with a **database,** have made changes you haven't yet saved, and have the option of ignoring the error, you should ignore the program error and then save the database. Do save the document by using a new **filename,** however. You don't want to replace the preceding version of the document with a new, possibly corrupted, version. After you've saved the document, close the program.

Other

Access Gives You an Error Message or Behaves Oddly

Access is a large, complex program. Sometimes files get corrupted, which can adversely affect its performance.

Run Detect And Repair

Choose the Help menu's Detect And Repair command to fix noncritical files, such as font files.

148

Quick Reference

Any time you explore a new
program, you're bound to
see features and tools you
can't identify. To be sure
you can identify the
commands and toolbar
buttons you see in
Microsoft Access, this
Quick Reference
describes these items in
systematic detail.

Database Window Menu Guide

File Menu

New...   Creates a new database. You specify the name of the database file and its location.

Open...   Retrieves an existing database from a floppy or hard disk.

Get External Data   Displays the Get External Database submenu.

> **Import...**   Imports a database object—such as a table— into the open database.

> **Link Tables...**   Connects an external data source to an Access database so that you can query the data source from inside Access.

Close   Closes the open database file or object.

Save   Saves the database object shown in the active document window.

Save As...   Saves the database object shown in the active document window, but with a new name and/or as a different object— table, query, form, or data access page

Export...   Exports the data in a database object to another program

Page Setup...   Describes how printed pages should look and lets you make changes to the way printed pages look.

Print Preview   Displays a window that shows how printed database objects look.

Print...   Prints the open database object.

Send To   Displays the Send To submenu.

> **Mail Recipient** Sends the selected object's data in an e-mail message.

> **Mail Recipient (As Attachment...)** Sends the selected object as an attachment to an e-mail message.

Database Properties   Gives you information about a database and lets you change some of that information.

Exit   Closes, or stops, the Access application.

About the numbered File menu commands

The File menu also provides numbered commands that identify the last four databases you opened. You can open one of these databases by choosing its numbered command.

Edit Menu

Undo	Reverses, or undoes, the last database object change.
Cut	Moves the current selection to the Clipboard.
Copy	Moves a copy of the current selection to the Clipboard.
Paste	Moves the Clipboard contents to the active database or object.
Create Shortcut...	Creates a shortcut icon for the selected database object.
Delete	Erases the current selection.
Rename	Changes the name of the selected database object.

Access menus are context sensitive

Access may add commands to a menu depending on the selected database object.

View Menu

Database Objects	Displays the Database Objects submenu.
Tables	Lists the table objects in the database.
Queries	Lists the query objects in the database.
Forms	Lists the form objects in the database.
Reports	Lists the report objects in the database.
Pages	Lists the data access page objects in the database.
Macros	Lists the macro objects in the database.
Modules	Lists the module objects in the database.
Large Icons	Displays database objects as large icons in the Database Window.

continues

151

View Menu *(continued)*

S_m_all Icons	Displays database objects as small icons in the Database Window.
L_i_st	Displays database objects in a list (the default view).
_D_etails	Displays database objects in a list that includes detailed descriptions of each object.
_A_rrange Icons	Displays the Arrange Icons submenu.

By _N_ame	Arranges database objects by name.
By _T_ype	Arranges database objects by type.
By _C_reated	Arranges database objects by creation date.
By _M_odified	Arranges database objects by last modification date.
_A_utoArrange	Automatically arranges database object icons and rearranges them every time you add or delete an object.

Line _U_p Icons	Arranges database object icons in neat, vertical columns.
_P_roperties	Displays information about the selected database object and lets you change that information.
_T_oolbars	Specifies which toolbars are shown and how they look, and displays the Toolbars submenu.

Clipboard	Displays the Clipboard toolbar.
Database	Toggles the Database toolbar on and off.
Web	Toggles the Web toolbar on and off.
_C_ustomize...	Displays the Customize dialog box to let you customize toolbars and menus.

Re_f_resh	Redraws the database window to reflect changes in the database structure.

Insert Menu

Table	Adds a new table object to the open database.
Query	Adds a new query object to the open database.
Form	Adds a new form object to the open database.
Report	Adds a new report object to the open database.
Page	Adds a new data access page object to the open database.
Macro	Adds a new macro object to the open database.
Module	Adds a new module object to the open database.
Class Module	Adds a new class module object to the open database.
AutoForm	Automatically creates a form for the selected table or query.
AutoReport	Automatically creates a report for the selected table or query.

Tools Menu

Spelling...	Checks spelling of the selected field.
AutoCorrect...	Lets you change the way AutoCorrect works and add to the list of corrections that AutoCorrect makes.
Office Links	Displays the Office Links submenu.
	Merge It With **MS Word** Exports data to a Microsoft Word table.
	Publish It With **MS Word** Exports data to a Rich Text File that Word can open.
	Analyze It With **MS Excel** Exports data to a Microsoft Excel workbook.
Online Collaboration	Displays the Online Collaboration submenu.
	Meet Now — Lets you enter information about yourself and your Internet directory so that others can find you.

continues

153

Tools Menu *(continued)*

Relationships... Lets you view and edit relationships between tables and queries.

Analyze Displays the Analyze submenu.

Table Normalizes your database by splitting tables.

Performance Fine-tunes your database to increase its speed.

Documenter Produces reports that describe database objects.

Database Utilities Displays the Database Utilities submenu.

Convert Database... Converts database from another application or a previous version of Access.

Compact And Repair Database Compacts database so that it takes up less disk space and fixes minor errors.

Linked Table Manager Lets you add and change connections to external data sources.

Database Splitter Moves tables from your database to a new, back-end database.

Switchboard Manager Edits your database switchboard objects.

Upsizing Wizard Upsizes your Access database to a Microsoft SQL Server Database.

Make MDE File... Saves a database as an MDE file.

Security Displays the Security submenu.

Set Database Password... Assigns a password to the open database.

User And Group Permissions... Describes what database users can do.

User And Group Accounts... Describes database users.

User-Level Security Wizard... Helps you set permission levels.

Encrypt/Decrypt Database... Codes or decodes database for security.

Replication   Displays the Replication submenu.

Synchronize Now... Synchronizes the current, selected replica with another replica.

Create Replica... Converts the current database to a design master and creates a replica database.

Partial Replica Wizard Creates a partial replica, by using only a portion of the current database's data.

Recover Design Master... Tells Access to consider the current replica as the design-master replica in a replica set.

Resolve Conflicts... Fixes any replication synchronization problems.

Startup...   Tells Access how it should open a database and how it should behave after the database is open.

Macro   Displays the Macro submenu.

Visual Basic Editor Creates or edits a macro.

Run Macro...   Starts a macro.

Convert Macros to Visual Basic... Converts the selected macro object to Visual Basic code.

Create Menu From Macro Creates a command menu from the selected macro object.

Create Toolbar From Macro Creates a toolbar from the selected macro object.

Create Shortcut Menu From Macro Creates a shortcut menu from the selected macro object.

ActiveX Controls...   Describes any custom control objects you want to use.

Add-Ins   Runs the Add-Ins Manager.

Customize...   Lets you customize toolbars and menus.

Options...   Lets you change the way Access works.

Window Menu

Tile Horizontally	Arranges the open document windows into horizontal tiles in a manner similar to the way ceramic tiles get arranged in a shower or bath.
Tile Vertically	Arranges the open document windows into vertical tiles.
Cascade	Arranges the open windows in a stack so that each window's title bar is visible.
Arrange Icons	Arranges the minimized window icons into neat little rows.
Hide	Removes the active object window from the Access application window.
Unhide...	Adds a previously hidden object window to the Access application window.
Size To Fit Form	Sizes the active window to fit the form in it.

About the numbered Window menu commands

The Window menu also lists as numbered commands the Database Window and any object windows. You can open a listed window by choosing the numbered command.

Help Menu

Microsoft Access Help	Starts the Office Assistant.
Hide/Show The Office Assistant	Hides the Office Assistant character or shows it, if hidden.
What's This?	Displays helpful information about whatever you click next: a menu command, a toolbar button, or an element of the Access application or object window.
Office On The Web	Connects you to a variety of Microsoft forums on the World Wide Web to get help with your questions.
Detect And Repair...	Automatically finds and fixes problems with Access.
About Microsoft Access	Displays the copyright notice, the software version number, and system information about your computer; also has a button you can click to get information about technical support for Access.

Standard Toolbar Buttons

Creates a new database file.

Displays the Open Database dialog box so that you can retrieve an existing database.

Saves any changes you made to your database.

Prints the active database object.

Shows what the printed pages of a database object will look like.

Checks the spelling of the selected field or fields.

Moves the current selection to the Clipboard.

Moves a copy of the current selection to the Clipboard.

Moves the Clipboard contents to the active database or object.

Copies formatting from one object to another.

Undoes the last change made to your database.

Displays a drop-down list box of tools you can use to move database objects to other Microsoft Office applications.

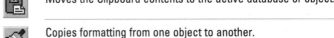

Displays a drop-down list box of tools you can use to normalize tables, improve database performance, and document database objects.

Opens the selected object in Visual Basic.

Opens a property sheet for the selected object.

Specifies table relationships.

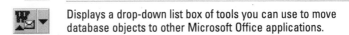

Displays a drop-down list box of tools you can use to add new objects.

Displays the Office Assistant animated help assistant.

Database Window Toolbar Buttons

 Opens the selected object in the Database Window.

 Opens the selected object in Design view in the Database Window.

 Opens a new object in the Database Window.

 Deletes the selected object in the Database Window.

 Tells Access to use large icons in the Database Window.

 Tells Access to use small icons in the Database Window.

 Tells Access to display a list of database objects in the Database Window.

 Tells Access to display a list of database objects along with descriptions in the Database Window.

Special Characters

A

B

C

E

Y

The manuscript for this book was prepared and submitted to Microsoft Press in electronic form. Text files were prepared using Microsoft Word 97. Pages were composed by Stephen L. Nelson, Inc., using PageMaker 6.5 for Windows, with text in Minion and display type in Univers. Composed pages were delivered to the printer as electronic prepress files.

Cover Designer
Tim Girvin Design, Inc.

Layout
Jeff Adell

Project Editor
Paula Thurman

Copy Editor
Rebecca Whitney

Writers
Geoff Miller and Steve Nelson

Technical Editor
Jessica Fiedelak

Indexer
Julie Kawabata

Printed on recycled paper stock.

See clearly—
now!

Here's the remarkable, *visual* way to quickly find answers about the powerfully integrated features of the Microsoft® Office 2000 applications. Microsoft Press AT A GLANCE books let you focus on particular tasks and show you, with clear, numbered steps, the easiest way to get them done right now. Put Office 2000 to work today, with AT A GLANCE learning solutions, made by Microsoft.

- MICROSOFT OFFICE 2000 PROFESSIONAL AT A GLANCE
- MICROSOFT WORD 2000 AT A GLANCE
- MICROSOFT EXCEL 2000 AT A GLANCE
- MICROSOFT POWERPOINT® 2000 AT A GLANCE
- MICROSOFT ACCESS 2000 AT A GLANCE
- MICROSOFT FRONTPAGE® 2000 AT A GLANCE
- MICROSOFT PUBLISHER 2000 AT A GLANCE
- MICROSOFT OFFICE 2000 SMALL BUSINESS AT A GLANCE
- MICROSOFT PHOTODRAW® 2000 AT A GLANCE
- MICROSOFT INTERNET EXPLORER 5 AT A GLANCE
- MICROSOFT OUTLOOK® 2000 AT A GLANCE

Microsoft®

mspress.microsoft.com

Microsoft Press offers *comprehensive* **learning solutions**
to help **new users, power users, and professionals** get the most from *Microsoft technology.*

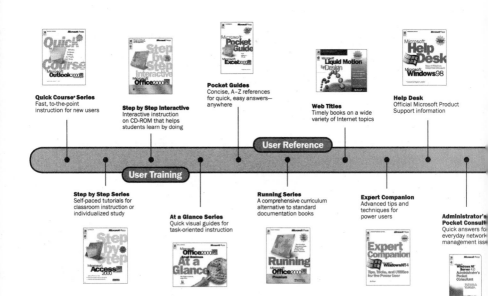

Quick Course® Series
Fast, to-the-point instruction for new users

Step by Step Interactive
Interactive instruction on CD-ROM that helps students learn by doing

Pocket Guides
Concise, A–Z references for quick, easy answers—anywhere

Web Titles
Timely books on a wide variety of Internet topics

Help Desk
Official Microsoft Product Support information

User Reference

User Training

Step by Step Series
Self-paced tutorials for classroom instruction or individualized study

At a Glance Series
Quick visual guides for task-oriented instruction

Running Series
A comprehensive curriculum alternative to standard documentation books

Expert Companion
Advanced tips and techniques for power users

Administrator's Pocket Consul
Quick answers for everyday network management issu

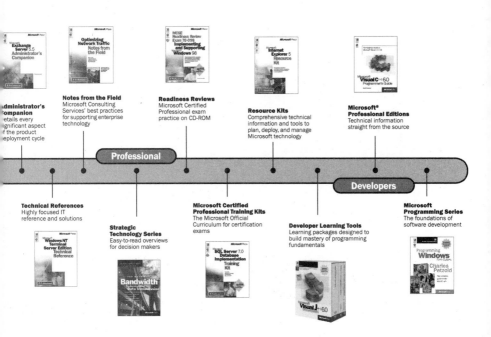

Stay in the *running* for maximum productivity.

These are *the* answer books for business users of Microsoft® Office 2000. They are packed with everything from quick, clear instructions for new users to comprehensive answers for power users—the authoritative reference to keep by your computer and use every day. THE RUNNING SERIES—learning solutions made by Microsoft.

- RUNNING MICROSOFT 2000 EXCEL 2000
- RUNNING MICROSOFT OFFICE 2000 PREMIUM
- RUNNING MICROSOFT OFFICE 2000 PROFESSIONAL
- RUNNING MICROSOFT OFFICE 2000 SMALL BUSINESS
- RUNNING MICROSOFT WORD 2000
- RUNNING MICROSOFT POWERPOINT® 2000
- RUNNING MICROSOFT ACCESS 2000
- RUNNING MICROSOFT INTERNET EXPLORER 5
- RUNNING MICROSOFT FRONTPAGE® 2000
- RUNNING MICROSOFT OUTLOOK® 2000